Journeys with the caterpillar:

Travelling through the mystical islands of Flores and Sumba, Indonesia

By Shivaji Das

The decision

Five out of over seventeen thousand and five hundred islands; Bali, Flores, Rinca, Komodo, and Sumba. We will be travelling for three weeks, most of the time to be spent in Flores and Sumba. That was the plan. Both Lobo and I were spoilt for choice. We could have gone to Syria and its mythical cities of Damascus, Aleppo and Homs, but the Saudis and Iranians were still continuing their proxy wars in its heartland. We could have gone to Nepal and taught our lungs and knees a lesson in its mountains, but the approaching rainy season would probably have left us spending all our time on merely finding ways to dry our wet clothes, one of my father's lifetime passions. And then there was Sichuan; but aren't we, the residents of dishwasher clean Singapore, well aware of public toilet horror stories in China? In other words, Indonesia promised to be the cheapest option.

The islands promised enough to be able to boast to colleagues and friends for a few minutes and elicit those vacuous, get-rid-of-him responses like, "Wow, you guys are so adventurous." I was hoping to watch Komodo Dragons in the wild give tourists chase. There could also be close encounters with flying lizards, flying fish, manta rays, and sand flies. The trip promised an excess of volcanoes, around seventeen of them. We could see the lakes in Kelimutu, Flores, that change colours every now and then. We would pass through traditional villages with elaborately roofed houses, surrounded by green hills, which were inhabited by animist societies in both Flores and Sumba, reputedly still following their ancient customs; funerals accompanied by ritualistic animal slaughters, megalithic tomb building, and fighting mock wars on horseback. On the internet, the pictures of the places we intended to visit looked good and made me want to take the same pictures.

We were about to get married in a couple of months. This would be our pre-honeymoon. In any case, we had no plans for honeymoon. But perhaps, this was also to be the final test; whether we can tolerate each other. Each day during this trip, we will be spending more time with each other during than we could expect in our normal workday lives. And these would be days spent without possibility of any luxury for based on our budget and our past experience in Indonesia, every aspect of our proposed trip, whether its stay, transport, or food, will be bereft of any typical traveller's sense of comfort. This was our last chance to say 'No', *'Niet', 'Na', 'Bu yao'*.

Getting a break for three weeks was not easy. What is just a 'whatever' in a universe over thirteen billion years old can be a reason for irreversible coma in the corporate world, with its self-reinforcing chants of 'twenty-four-by-seven'. Lobo was in the process of changing jobs and so was in a rather comfortable situation in this regard. As for me, it took some preparation to confront my boss with this proposition.

I decided to pursue my well proven 'toilet stealth' strategy. Toilets are instrumental for career progression. They are usually the only place for faceless juniors to access their super-bosses. Urinating next to a boss is a great opportunity to mumble sweet nothings; interest in the company's recent performance, a few mundane but passionate suggestions about potential opportunities, followed by balladeering praise of the super-boss's recent 'state of the company' speech. Follow it up with your humble request and there are very good chances that it would be granted. But beware; don't even think of checking on the super-boss's masculinity at such moments.

This significance of office toilets in corporate life results in a vicious circle for female employees. After all, in most economies, the super-bosses are usually male, and even if there are sufficient females among the super-bosses, the cubicle structure of ladies' toilets make them rather unsuitable for this strategy. The women can only hope that someone other than Gorbachev brings down those walls.

So I matched my circadian rhythm with my boss. And as soon as I saw my boss take that elegant turn for the toilet, I rushed in. A few niceties and soon I positioned my leave application as a selfless exercise purely sought for the benefit of the organisation. I told him, "My shrewdly planned absence will force my team to grow and make leaders out of them." I took an oath, "I will seek new business opportunities in Indonesia even when on leave." I promised, "I will be available over phone and email, twenty four by seven of course." And then I dropped the fusion bomb, "I have been inspired to embark on this after reading about Steve Job's trip to India." After all, how can any sane person stop someone from doing something similar to what Steve Jobs had done? If the word got out that he denied me leave, my boss's job would be on the line. As my rambling went on and on, my boss started fidgeting. Obviously, he didn't want to linger for too long surrounded by urinals. "Ok, it's fine," he sped away as I dried my hands with great content.

For trip preparations, I offered to plan the itinerary, transport and lodging. Lobo, instinctively, offered to do the necessary shopping; the clothes, the raincoats, and the luggage. That was a dangerous prospect, for Lobo, who spent her early years in mainland China, retains a worldview that is still in some ways influenced by the mainland. And there, the idea of proper dressing for male tourists implies being always prepared to attend a wedding that is happening in the 1980s. So even if one expects to be spending all his time on a tropical beach, he should always be wearing formal shoes, loose trousers that reach up to the chest, and a plain colored half-sleeve shirt that should imply that the person is forty years older than he actually is. He should also always wear a heavy money bag at his waist so that at any moment, he could replace the ticket collector in a public bus. But I had just got engaged to Lobo, so I had little choice in this regard. Nonetheless, she bought me stuff which I couldn't really object to. One t-shirt had bold Chinese writing on the back, "Number 1 scholar in China". I could live with that.

When it came to my area of responsibility, I turned again to the testament, the internet. We planned to take a flight from Singapore to Bali and then another to the island of Flores. Our first stop in Flores would be the port city of Labuan Bajo. From Labuan Bajo, we would be visiting Rinca and Komodo islands using an overnight boat. Subsequently, we would head for the hill town of Ruteng, reported by some as the dirtiest town in the world, from where we would trek to the isolated traditional village of Wae Rebo. The next destination would be another hill town, Bajawa, and the traditional villages in its surroundings. From there, we would go to the port city of Ende, the town closest to the three coloured lakes of Kelimutu. From Ende, we hoped to take a ship or ferry to the island of Sumba. At this point, it became quite difficult to plan as no source could confidently tell us which day the ship or ferry left from Ende for Sumba. So I decided to figure out this part of the trip only after we reached Ende. All I knew was that somehow we would have to reach the port town of Waingapu in East Sumba and then take the bus to Waikabubak in West Sumba, where we would spend a week visiting some more traditional villages before coming back to Bali by flight and then to Singapore.

There were all sorts of opinions from the few people who had cared to visit Flores and Sumba and then write about them on the world wide web. Most complained about the lack of hot shower facilities. One guy was so pleased with the only hot shower he could get, at some hotel in a town called Ruteng, that he posted pictures of himself in the shower. The sight of that bald guy happily taking a hot shower was further confirmation that our choice of the islands for the trip was just right.

It was also my duty to get the medicines. Those who cared to write on the internet forums, glory be to them, advised carrying a Mount Uluru-sized pile of medicines. I shortlisted the diseases I would not mind having and approached the friendly neighbourhood doctor for cures for the rest. Since Lobo was busy with her shopping, she passed on to me her own shortlist of diseases. Lobo was particularly concerned about her nose. Her nose is indeed one of the wonders of nature that could and should influence biomimetics. It is extremely sensitive to even the slightest variations in temperature and wind, indicating these variations happily with a machine gun flurry of sneezes. Unfortunately, her nose is at steady state only under vacuum at a temperature of around forty degree Celsius. This means that she starts firing at the slightest hint of air conditioning, fan, rain, a daft of strong wind, or even a gentle breeze from a mosquito's wing-flapping. In addition, she would also fire when she was hungry or if she had been stationary for too long. Pretending to be the owner of such a mystical nose in front of the friendly neighbourhood doctor was never going to be the ideal way to spend an evening. On hearing the peculiarities of Lobo's nose, which was now my nose, the doctor expressed surprise in earnest seriousness. He inspected my nose from all angles thoroughly. He held it for a while and moved it like a gearbox lever. He tapped on it. He came closer and for a moment, I wondered if he intended to take a dive into the pair of cosmic black holes. He sat for a while holding his forehead. He walked back and forth in the room. He did something on his computer, perhaps a search on Google. Eventually, he settled down and gave me a few anti-histamines. I accepted his offer without asking any questions hoping to get out of this act as soon as possible to move on to the main item on the agenda, malaria.

I had already done all my research on the internet. So when the doctor prescribed a medicine, I immediately asked if it was Lariam. "It is Larium," he mumbled, avoiding eye-contact with me. I knew already that Lariam can bring about nightmares and psychotic behaviour. One report mentioned a Lariam-doused lady taking off all her clothes in a van during her thousand-dollars-a-night Kenyan safari and screaming names of dead people. Some even used it for recreational purposes. I asked the doctor for the alternative, Doxycycline, and he happily obliged. I wonder why he preferred to recommend Lariam in the first place. I had a feeling that it had something to do with my nose, or shall we say Lobo's nose.

The day we were to take off kept coming nearer and nearer till the earth was suddenly at such a point along its axes for rotation and revolution that we had to eventually flag down a taxi for the airport. For the second time in my life, I accidentally took a police car to be a taxi and raised my hand. And for the second time in my life, the policemen inside the car were sensible enough to take me for a weird creature,, ignore me and pass by.

Once we cleared the immigration and check-in niceties, both Lobo and I took out our writing pads. But I found it hard to write anything yet. I was hoping to describe sunsets and sunrises much better than anyone has ever done before. I was hoping to describe landscapes with language that, for the first time, did justice to each glorious fold of the hills and each splendid bend in the river. And most of all, I was hoping to write about people from these places and reveal those hidden corners of humanity that I thought were still hidden from every one of us. I intended to write about this trip with an excellence that no travel writer had achieved yet. The loud boarding announcements cracked in. Our journey had begun.

A frog's hop from Bali to Labuan Bajo

The flight was uneventful as most flights are. The only pleasure I get from flights nowadays is to order for a special meal in advance, in this case, a Jain meal. That means no meat, no eggs, no fish, no onions, no garlic, no ginger, and nothing with roots; in other words, something that would create some harassment for the airlines. Now, while I was indeed attempting a conversion to vegetarianism, I am not a Jain myself and have no elevated sympathy for vegetables that prefer to grow underground. However, there is a certain pleasure I take in causing a little bit more harassment to any airline, those monsters who love to charge extra for additional underwear in my bag. And a vegetarian maestro had once guided me, "You always get your food first, while the others around you can only smell and look."

I had been to Bali two years ago. But this time around, things looked a lot busier. There seemed to be overwhelmingly more tourists. In particular, there were endless queues of Chinese tourists travelling in large groups atthe visa-on-arrival counters. Later, I learnt that the film *Eat, Pray and Love* had done wonders for tourism in Bali. I also learnt that the Chinese had overtaken the Japanese as the second largest source of tourists to Bali, with Australia being number one. I observed a nanosecond of silence for the Japanese, to offer my condolences for them being overtaken in everything nowadays.

Our stay in Bali was short, at a homestay owned by Mr. Ketut and our only day there was spent enjoying the views of the surrounding rice fields in the morning and then visiting the water palace at Tirta Gangga. The room at Ketut's place had an impressive toilet. After it was flushed, it always gave out a long wail, like an ambulance alarm only a lot more mournful. It seemed to ask, "Is this my fate? And is this how you treat me? And you call yourself civilised people?"

The next day, we took the flight in a regional airline to the town of Labuan Bajo in Flores. The plane was small, a propeller-driven with a capacity of around thirty seats, the kind of planes that still manage to maintain their passengers in a somewhat happy and relaxed mood. And so it was, even though the flight was rather full. One middle-aged man caught my attention. He was unusually red, a shade lighter than that of a watermelon, very uniformly baked. He had an exuberant grin on his face, like someone who had indeed been rescued from a grill.

Soon after take-off, a couple, two seats ahead of us, started making out rather ferociously. While yawning and clapping are contagious for biological reasons, making out is fast becoming contagious out of social compulsion. How can our relationship be less passionate than theirs? Are we already ebbing out? How far are we from realising the truth? Or have we already… That's why couples who make out in public are always disgusting for others around them. The man looking like the grilled chicken was the first to give in and started making out with his partner. Another couple in front of us gave in. Two nuns, also on the flight, kept looking intensely at the dining tray folded at the back of the seat in front of them. I tried to see if that technique worked and, lo, behold, there was this printed on the dining tray, 'Activating mobile phone during flight will result in a penalty of two years' imprisonment and a fine of Rupiah two hundred million.' It seemed a punishment worthy of genocide and was just appropriate a topic to divert Lobo's attention from those onerous questions about relationships surrounded by a whirlpool of couples infected with the making-out bug.

As we looked out of the window, we saw samples from the Ring of Fire for which Indonesia is well known. First came the volcano Mount Batur in Bali with its giant caldera and the shiny lake inside it. Soon we were flying over the island of Lombok and the three islands of Gili forming three gentle teardrops. Slowly we came over the volcano Mount Rinjani and its beautiful crater lake. The year before, we had climbed Mount Rinjani and the view of the summit, the surrounding valleys and the lake with a new cone emerging from within the lake, left us both with a sense of meeting again someone we loved and respected. I stretched my neck to catch a last glimpse of the lake and soon we were over the island of Sumbawa, where Adolf Hitler is rumoured to have escaped to. From Sumbawa rose the enormous volcano known as Mount Tambora. It looked beautiful from above, the wrinkled skin of the mountain circling up the jagged edges of the giant rim, an elegant monster with a flair for cuddling soft white clouds. Mount Tambora is supposed to have been responsible for the most powerful eruption in recorded history. The three active volcanoes, Mount Batur, Mount Rinjani and Mount Tambora, each having unleashed its own ravishing power at different times in history, were now meditating in a line. Three sisters, sleeping, with their jaws open; fluffy clouds gently climbing over them; and deep inside, the hot, red and thick liquid gently nudging the doors to open so it can see the skies and become a rock again. Soon we crossed the Wallace line, the boundary between Asian and Australian animal species. I had read before that among mammals, only long tailed macaques had bothered to cross the line. Including Lobo and I, around thirty no-tailed apes were doing the crossing now. And what prompted the long tailed ones to cross the line?

After an hour's flight, we landed in Labuan Bajo, Flores. Flores, Flores, Flores, what a beautiful name for an island, after the Portuguese word for flowers! I have always liked Indonesian names and the names of Javanese towns and landmarks such as Surakarta, Probolinggo Wonosobo, and Malioboro always tickled my tongues and ears whenever I read them or spelt them out. The names in Flores sound different but have a certain earthy charm to them: Labuan Bajo, Bajawa, Ngade, Larantuka. My favourite is Larantuka with its hint of grace and earth. I told Lobo that if we ever have a daughter, we should name her Larantuka.

When we finally landed in Labuan Bajo, I kept chanting in my mind, Flores, Flores, Flores. Flores appears on the map like a young whale, bloated towards the west, narrowing down with a rather jaunty tail pointing upwards. Except for the coasts, the topography is mountainous with sixteen volcanoes scattered from the east to the west forming Flores' share of the Indonesian ring of fire. Such difficult topography meant that there was relatively scant settlement along Flores except for its coasts. As a consequence, the place didn't seem to have much of a written history before the Portuguese arrived here in the sixteenth century. It is one of those places where people had lived for many thousands of years but hadn't bothered to record their legacy. What if such places had at one time witnessed the kind of human scheming and graft unimaginable in any other civilization to date? What if the gravest sins and massacres had once been committed in such places? And what if the people of Flores at one time had the most humane form of social structure, the most refined form of a legal system and the most ideal way of dealing with the inequalities at birth? We will never know.

What we do know is that even before the Portuguese had arrived, people from north and south Sulawesi had set up small settlements along the coasts. There may also have been settlements from neighbouring Sumba islands. And once the Portuguese arrived, they immediately set about converting the local people. It was still a slow process and while Larantuka and places in the east of Flores have had a history of Christianity for over four hundred years, Christianity in the central and western parts of this rugged mountainous island is only a hundred years old. There were recorded events of struggle and skirmishes for power between the local powers, the Portuguese and the Dutch until the 1850s when a Portuguese governor, for want of money, sold parts of Flores to the Dutch East India Company. The governor was apparently disowned and dismissed by the Portuguese back in Lisbon but for some reason, they decided to honour the deal and Flores, in its entirety, became a part of the Dutch East Indies. After independence, Flores continued to trail behind Java, Bali and the more accessible or resource-rich parts of Indonesia in terms of economic development. As of now, while tourism is emerging as a driving force of the economy's growth, the economy remains dependent on small-scale agriculture with most of the islanders hoping to get a government job as a way out of poverty.

Labuan Bajo was hot and dry. At the airport, there were pictures of Komodo dragons everywhere and for a tourist, Labuan Bajo seemed to exist only to push him over to Komodo country. In the posters, the Komodo dragons were in very glamorous settings. One was posing in front of a secluded beach. One was looking at a sunset. Before this, I had seen one lonely female in Singapore zoo and it didn't appear particularly impressive or menacing. And I was sceptical of the ferocious image portrayed by the nature-shows on television since they are used to hype any physical trait of the animals they had managed to make a film on. I had read that it was possible to visit Komodo and Rinca islands in small boats and then sleep over at night. More than the dragons, it was the possibility of the stars in the remoteness that I was interested in.

The taxi drivers outside the airport were quoting atrocious prices, enough to take us back to Bali. After we managed to get out of their clutches, we met two innocent-looking ojek (motorcycle) drivers who were less aware of purchasing power parities. The two turned out to be brothers. Within five minutes, we reached the hotel that was the first on the way to town, Chez Felix. At first glance, Chez Felix appeared to be a clothes-dryer's paradise. Clothes were drying everywhere, in front of every room, in the garden , in the restaurant overlooking the sea and Rinca Island. Looking at them, I realized that men's underwear came in a wide range of sizes, from being able to trap a fly to one meant to catch a grizzly bear. Later we would realise that places with such sunshine were rare in Flores and tourists coming from elsewhere must have jumped at the first opportunity to strip down and start washing. As soon as we got our room, Lobo decided to start washing as well.

The rooms in Chez Felix were born out of an inspiring architectural vision; a vision inspired by hospital rooms, school classrooms and small town churches. The color on the wall was a sky blue I had often seen in government hospitals in India. Two melancholy posters of Jesus and

Mary kept staring at the bed with floral prints. A small fan hung in the centre of the room and kept rotating, looking like an American spy prop, keeping an eye on the world.

Labuan Bajo is hardly more than a fishing village with a small port. A road loops around most of this town, for a while going along the sea, then climbing up to the hills and then falling back again to the sea. The public transport in the form of bemos or minivans and ojeks therefore keeps following this circular route in one direction. The hills fall rather abruptly to the coast. Along the coast, one can see the several dry islands and their hills jutting out in various shapes across the quaint sea. It is a hot place and during the day, the town is largely taking a nap or watching television.

As soon as we stepped out, I realized that I needed to dress up like an Arab. But Arab dresses are not very suitable for travelling light as a backpacker so I had made my own rendition of an Arab contraption. I wound a scarf around my face from under the chin to the top of the head like a headscarf that left only my eyes and nose visible and then wore a cap on top of it to keep it in place. The result made me look less like an Arab and more like a black magic woman hiding from the eyes of the suspicious society. Armed and ready, we began walking down the hills from Chez Felix to the coast along a trail behind small houses with people sleeping under their elevated roofs.

We asked for directions at a house. The man woke up from his slumber to tell Lobo, "You are very beautiful". His young daughter, probably six or seven years old, commanded us, "Follow me," and led the way in jumping steps. All the people we met along the way greeted us with big smiles. Lobo was already feeling rather high in the face of Indonesian hospitality.

At the northern end of Labuan Bajo, along the coast, was the *Pasar* or market. The Pasar had been colonised by dry fish. Rows and rows of dried fish in cubist representation, split along their body axis and then spread out, the two halves still joined along the dorsal fin. Beyond the pasar, along the seafront, were a few dive shops, some tour agencies, and a handful of small stores. Within fifteen minutes of walking, we reached the end of the town as it climbed up again to the hills. The skyline of Labuan Bajo was dominated by washing lines which ran from anywhere to everywhere. The stiff and colourful clothes from these lines fluttered like Tibetan flags.

The heat was now overtaking our initial enthusiasm and we rushed inside a Padang-style restaurant. For some reason, Indonesia has a fascination with Padang restaurants. In such restaurants, ten to twenty different items are stacked up one above another in five or six columns in front of the restaurant window. The items on display are typical; deep fried beancurd (*tahu*), deep fried soybean cakes (*tempe*), deep fried chicken, deep fried fish, deep fried beef, deep fried boiled eggs, deep fried omelette, deep fried leaves in batter, and a vegetable curry with little vegetable inside. From the outside, it looks like a feast and at first sight, one can get restless about what to choose and what not to. We ordered too much. It came with a small serving of rice and a bigger serving of chilli paste. But soon, we struggled to finish most of this deep fried abundance. Our plates were nicely coated with cooking oil and I could already sense that Lobo was planning to skip many meals to make up for this. While the fried fish and fried chicken and the fried beancurd lay barely nibbled in our table, other people in the restaurant seemed to be in the spirit of Roman feasts. Their hands were digging into the fried fish with great momentum and purpose. They raised their heads from time to time in a synchronous manner and then laughed loudly among themselves before digging in again with even greater purpose. We looked around like helpless strangers and decided that the rice and the chilli paste were the healthiest options. We dug in the rice and the chilli and when we raised our heads in sync, two brave men, drenched in sweat, Calcifer unleashed from our tongues. The young owner of the restaurant who handed out such sinful exuberance was rather thin and he took a special interest in us. We started talking. "You should go to Komodo and Rinca using a fisherman's boat rather than a tour package. It would be far cheaper," he said. "I could ask around among my contacts and try to hook you up with someone later in the night." Excited at this proposition, we stepped out but immediately came up against the fury of the sun. The whole town was almost deserted by now.

We got out of the road to walk along the coast. Close to the shore, we came across a large platform that jutted out into the sea like a jetty. It was made of long bamboos and seemed to be very fragile. There, a few fishermen were spreading out their catch for drying in the same cubist formation as we had seen in the Pasar. Back on the coast, there were some more fish for drying, these ones not in a cubist formation.

The name Labuan Bajo means a port for the Bajo people, the sea-gypsies from Sulawesi. The gypsies have been travelling from Sulawesi to Flores for thousands of years. But even in recent years many men migrated to Labuan Bajo from Makassar in Sulawesi. Unlike most

Florenese, who were Christians, these Sulawesi men are Muslims and have married local women from Labuan Bajo. As such, the population of Labuan Bajo is evenly split between Muslims and Christians with the Muslims staying mostly along the coast and the Christians occupying the hills above. Perhaps as a result of their drive to outnumber each other, the town has been witnessing one of the highest population growth in Flores. Young children are everywhere, walking along the shady trail from the hills to the coast; sleeping in big groups under the raised floors of the houses; surrounding the television sets like an atoll. Every young woman has a cloth contraption holding a baby around her shoulders. Such population growth calls for more chickens and more eggs. So there is a matching abundance of mother chickens and their chicks as well in Labuan Bajo.

On the way back to Chez Felix, we found the point where the trail from the hills met the coastal road and continued walking up. But an old couple on the way gave us the friendly advice to take another branching trail. Half an hour of walking and we were still looking for the hotel. We came across a mother chicken which was tied to a pole. So when we came closer to inspect it and its babies, the mother inflated her posterior to hide all the babies inside. She kept on looking at us; her eyes frozen in fear as if the greatest misfortune had befallen her. We left after taking pity on the baby chicken, for their bomb shelter must have been rather smelly. An hour later, we were still looking for Chez Felix. In this incredibly small town, getting lost was even more incredible. I asked for directions from a lady chopping firewood in front of her rather isolated house. She became rather excited and asked me to go several directions at once. What I understood from her advice was that we should be taking a right from her place. At the same time, she kept pointing towards the left. I started wondering whether I remembered correctly the Indonesian words for left and right. Now, while I always take pride in being able to speak some basic Bahasa Indonesia, and Lobo absolutely admires me for that, in reality, I knew only a handful of words. So in many conversations, I would start off boldly with the usual greetings, the words and sentences I was very comfortable with, and my perfect accent for those initial words would end up giving the listener and Lobo a false sense of confidence. In fact, within the first two sentences, after I have already said, *"Kami dari Singapura, saya asal dari India, dia asal dari China* (We are from Singapore, I am originally from India, she is originally from China), the listener has already complimented me for my excellent Bahasa Indonesia. Hearing this, I reply feigning humility, *"sedikit sedikit saja"*, (little little only). This further establishes me as a maestro of the language. But soon after, my sentences would say farewell to the rules of grammar. My choice of words would be rather incorrect and my hand gestures will gradually take over the act of communicating from my mouth. At this point, the listener would be rather confused. Not just because what I was saying would stop making much sense, but also given my initial bold and confident start, the listener would be still compelled to give me the benefit of the doubt. Perhaps he would take me to be an abstract philosopher speaking in cryptic language. Or perhaps I would be saying something that he, with his limited knowledge, was not able to comprehend. Lobo, in the meantime, still keeps having faith in me because she is convinced that the listener speaks a dialect different from the pure Javanese that I am more conversant with. But deep in my heart, I knew that at that moment in Labuan Bajo, I was trying to remember what stood for left and what stood for right.

After wandering around for a bit more, we finally decided to flag down a *bemo* or min-van to take us to Chez Felix. And that is where we met the Caterpillar. The caterpillar is everywhere in Flores and Sumba and occasionally in Bali too. It has bright big eyes. A big smile runs through its face, like the one in those "Service with a smile" badges. It has soft padded legs and two soft padded antennae. It likes to lie down across the dashboard of cars. Most of these caterpillars are candyfloss pink in colour, though I also came across some red and orange ones. For some reason, all bemo drivers in Flores and Sumba like to have these stuffed toys along with them and throughout our journey, these caterpillars would be our constant companion.

Once the sun went down, the road along the seafront in Labuan Bajo wakes up before going to sleep again after two hours. There are even a few touts looking for tourists to sell a diving trip or a trip to Komodo Island. "Take my boat, mine is the only boat that has a western toilet," screamed one.

We managed to get a deal for a two-day trip to Komodo and Rinca Islands from a small tour shop run by Louis and Marcel. Louis is a man of fifty and he claims to have been one of the first English-speaking tour guides in Labuan Bajo. He said, "I had gone to Bali to work in a hotel and learn English," a story rather common to many people in Flores. "Thereafter, I had worked in the kitchens in Jakarta and Surabaya." He showed us pictures of kids surrounding him and a foreign tourist, "These were taken during my trip to the isolated village of Wae Rebo. I was the first guide to Wae Rebo. When we had reached there, the kids couldn't control themselves in excitement."

The trip was to begin early in the morning when a small boat would take us to a few islands including Rinca and Komodo. At these two islands, we would be able to do some trekking to see the dragons. At certain points in the sea, we could go snorkelling. One night would be spent on the boat itself and the crew would prepare all the meals. We would be the only people in the boat other than the two-man crew. Marcel, the twenty-something assistant of Louis, asked us what kind of food we would like to have on the boat. Fresh from our deep-fried Padang encounter, we asked for vegetables, an awful lot of vegetables.

Along the road, we came across a wedding celebration. In a small enclosure lit with bright fluorescent tubes, about a hundred people had assembled. A bunch of musicians were seated at the centre. A fat blind man was playing the organ. Sitting next to him, a middle-aged lady was singing over a loud microphone. At the centre, a bunch of young men were dancing with slow pelvic thrusts. Their eyes closed, the men appeared to be deep in love with one another. At times, they synchronised their pelvic thrusts. People took turns to come to the centre stage and dance. Hired young girls, looking rather bored, joined the fray. The young men danced around them, showering them with small notes. There was too much smoke in the air from the cigarettes and as we took our leave, a bunch of teenagers approached us. One of them asked in English, "Mister, where are you from? I am from Indonesia."

Within a breath of the Komodos

Early next morning, Marcel was at the hotel with a bemo and the caterpillar to take us down to the jetty. Perhaps this was the high level of customer service that Marcel and Louis swore by or perhaps it was their strategy to ensure that we didn't go with any other operator.

Once we reached the jetty, Lobo wanted to do some last-minute shopping, some bread to feed the fish when we would be snorkelling. Now, we are quite famous for being miserly in the marine fish community. Whenever we have gone snorkelling, for some reason we have never had anything to offer the fish from our own stock. But the sea has always reminded us to have good manners. At Krabi, we found a floating plastic bottle with a thin strand of bread inside it. With so little to spare, we held the bread in our fists just exposing a little, bit by bit, for the fish to nibble on. The fish there assumed the bread to be a real gourmet meal for it to be hidden and served in this fashion and so came to us in hordes abandoning the other floating tourists. We managed to make that bread piece last for over half an hour. At the Gili islands in Lombok, we were fortunate to see another piece of bread floating inside a small plastic bag. We adopted the same strategy but this time the fish were less keen to follow our 'small portions, healthy portions' policy. So we had to let go of bigger chunks and the bread was over within two minutes. This time around, Lobo was determined to be a proper guest. I obliged and moved to buy a big packet of bread but then she spotted that it was chocolate flavoured. "How can we serve such high sugar food to the poor fish?" she dismayed. She reminded me of diabetes, hypertension, impotency, sleep apnea and a long list of chronic diseases that humans get from obesity which she insisted the fish would also contract the moment they nibbled at that bread. I looked at the bread again and I saw a dozen dead fish, their faces lined with a layer of brown bread crust. I threw the bread back with disgust as if I may have contracted obesity just by holding it for a while. Unfortunately, all the bread in that shop, the most famous and only bakery in Labuan Bajo, were of sweet flavour. We looked around a few grocery stores and none of them had bread without sugar. After looking all around the town, I offered a suggestion to get some vitamin pills instead for the fish. Lobo took my advice and came back to the most famous and only bakery. We debated for a while on whether we should take the chocolate flavoured, pandan flavoured, or the cheese flavoured bread. The chocolate bread I had so despised just a few minutes ago, won.

The boat was sturdier than we had imagined. Largely made of wood, it was about ten metres in length and about four metres wide at its centre. The front of the boat was open along the sides and a shade was on top. There were two wooden benches along the sides and a wooden table at the centre. The captain's deck was at the back where there were arrangements for two people to crouch and sleep. There was a little space just behind this for the crew to cook and a small toilet at one corner. It was possible to climb on to the tin covered top of the deck through a basic ladder. The interiors were painted in lime green and the exteriors were all white. In front of the captain's deck was written the name of the boat, Fitra Mandiri.

The crew comprised of a father and son duo. The father had sharp features with taut weather-beaten skin. He was very lean and short and looked a lot younger than the fifty years he claimed to have lived. He was wearing a bright yellow cap with 'Rusty' written in front. He introduced himself as Captain Rudy. The son was about four feet tall, probably in his early teens. He was very lean as well and sported a dash of a rebel about him with stern looks and a tuft of long hair at the back of his head, a style quite popular among Indonesian youth. But his chubby cheeks went against this image he was trying to craft. When Marcel introduced us to them, the father-son duo seemed a little guarded. Without much small talk, they wanted to get on with their tasks immediately. Clumsily, we got onboard and the boat's motor began its lazy humming. It was a bright day and the sea was the colour of ink inside an inkpot.

Rinca appeared rather close but to our surprise, Captain Rudy said that it would take two hours for us to reach there. The boat moved slowly even though the sea was rather gentle. Soon we were surrounded by lime green hills. In the bright sun, the sea, the hills and the sky provided deep contrasts. The breeze was strong yet warm; ideal conditions for Lobo's nose and she became very excited and kept moving from one corner of the boat to another to catch all the glimpses this part of nature had to offer. Guides on travel writing that I had consulted before had all strongly advised using phrases such as azure sea or cobalt blue sea. So instead of joining Lobo, I began wondering how else to convey my sense of wonder at that place.

The islands all around us appeared rather arid with their small hills uniformly carpeted with the lime green rough looking grass. We came across one hill that had a lone tree at the top. Another stretch of grassy hills had a line of trees only at the top as if the trees decided to climb up from wherever they were born to settle down in a line at the top to enjoy the best vantage point. Suddenly in the middle of the sea, there was a large patch of bright green floating mangroves. At some stretches, mangroves lined the border between the sea and the hills and on that bright sunny day, the old yellow leaves mixed among the bright green gave an impression of a delightful garden tended to by the sea to greet the boats with shining lights lit up even in broad daylight. There was not a sight of civilization bar an occasional small boat coming from the other side. And after an hour of being on the slow moving boat, the sea gently rippling around us surrounded by the lime hills, I felt like this is how life has been for me every day; this is what I see around me all the time, these are the only people I know, this backpack is all the possession I have and this is how it will stay for as long as I will live.

After two hours of sailing, we docked at a point called Loh Buaya in Rinca Island, the second largest island in Komodo National Park and the one closest to Flores. It was time for me to take out my camera from the backpack and it took some digging to locate it. During this trip, I realised that the inside of a backpack is a world of its own. Calm, lifeless and rather dumb from outside, the backpack's inside is a battlefield with intense rivalries. Things churn, and the things that one needs the least always turns up right at the top while the ones you need the most are gradually pushed and shoved by the rest to the bottom. So whenever I fumble through my backpack, by some miracle, the nasty used underwear invariably turns up first. Then comes up all the tons of books that I carried along for no reason because there was no way I would be finishing even half of those even if I kept reading non-stop for the next three weeks, skipping sleep. So every time I opened my backpack, I had to send these eager front benchers back to the bottom. But I know that once I zip it up, intense negotiations will begin inside, invisible arms and legs will nudge past each other and the used underwear will creep right up.

As we walked to the park management office in Rinca, a smartly dressed young man carrying a forked stick approached us. "I am Adi and I will be your guide," he declared. After paying the necessary fees at the office which included the fixed and mandatory guide fees, we set off on the trail. We came across a stretch of land where many mangrove saplings had been recently planted. There were small cardboard signs on small wooden sticks next to each of these saplings with names of people and their country of origin and a year written on them. When we asked Adi about those boards, he said, "Those are the names of people killed by the Komodo dragons. They didn't bother to take guides and look what happened to them." There seemed to be one too many of these saplings and upon sensing our disbelief, he revealed, "Don't worry, those were names of people who had planted those saplings under a conservation programme." Pity those well-wishers who are now being commemorated as jokes on this island! Within minutes of walking, we came across a baby dragon running around, worry written all over its eyes. Adi became very excited, "It is very rare to see baby Komodos. They always live on the trees. You are very lucky," typical tourist guide phrases.

There are around three thousand dragons left in the world and just under half of them are in Rinca. Komodo Island had the largest population while some parts of Flores and the surrounding islands had only a handful. The Komodos have been known to the outside world only since 1910 and despite facing the threat of extinction owing to loss of natural habitats, were doing rather well in Komodo and Rinca because of their protected status. The local population, largely comprising convicts who had been once exiled from the nearby island of Sumbawa, revered the dragons and had a habit of feeding the dragons, a practice now non-existent because of government regulations. The dragons can reach up to three metres and weigh seventy kilogrammes with the males being considerably larger than the females. "Like humans, the Komodo eggs took eight to nine months to give a baby," said Adi. All the same, Adi made much of the fact that Komodo mothers were very different from human mothers, "Instead of nagging their kids all their lives with constant 'Why do this and why do that', they eat their newborn at the first opportunity." The hapless babies therefore resort to all sorts of tricks. "Some babies rub themselves in buffalo shit so that their mother doesn't want to eat him." Most give a dash and climb a tree as soon as they are out of their shells.

Adi also sounded solemn about the human deaths from Komodo bites. "One old tourist was killed a couple of years back while a child from the village on Rinca had been killed a decade ago." Adi was getting more and more melancholic, "Women having periods better avoid visiting the Komodos because with their keen sense of smell, they might come chasing for the blood." Just when I thought Adi would begin blaming the Komodos for global warming, we came across the park kitchen with a dozen dragons slumbering under and around the stilted house. Adi claimed, "These are pensioner Komodos, old lazy hags hoping to get easy food from a kind cook."

These Komodos looked uninterested in anyone around. There were seven of them, some females. They were far from any anthropomorphic idea of beauty. Even if they preferred to eat only spirulina, no one would probably cuddle them like the panda. Their dotted dark brown skin had many wrinkles and at their neck, the skin was heavily folded, making the head appear like a giant uncircumcised penis. Their big claws were hooked and pointed. An inverted smile adorned their faces, like a constant pout from a century-old grumpy grandmother. They were surrounded by tourists who were gasping at every small move the Komodos were making; a flick of the long forked yellow tongue, a gentle nudge from their hind legs, a slow fall of a thick lump of saliva from one's upper teeth, or a menacing slow turn of the neck to look right into someone's eyes. One of the first things guides tell you about the Komodos is their ability to outrun humans over short distance, and that possibility was probably playing on everyone's minds, tourists, guides as well as the Komodos.

But there are some aspects of a Komodo's appearance and attitude that were redeeming for them from an anthropomorphic point of view. They have a particularly adorable way of lying down with their small baby-like chubby hands and legs spread out perpendicular to their bodies. This makes it appear as if the Komodos are somehow grappling on to an earth that they know is constantly rotating and that things are not as stable as they appear. And with their rather endearingly round black and shiny eyes, they seem to appeal to everyone around to join them in lying down and holding on to the ground.

"Tell me some similarities between Komodos and you," said Adi. We were dumbstruck. "They suffer from bad breath, just like us," he grinned. Since the teeth of the Komodos are covered with gum tissue and they have a habit of heavy grinding, their sixty-odd teeth always bleed whenever they eat, reportedly causing the stinking dragon fire breath. Of course, this ever bleeding mouth also helps Komodos by providing prime property for all the bacteria that give their bite the toxic menace. "Tell me one more similarity," Adi the teacher stopped and looked back at us sharply. We gave him blank looks. "They are monogamous just like us, well maybe not me," he laughed out loud. "But you see, there are three males for every female Komodo here and the females can produce babies asexually. So imagine you", he pointed at me, "After fighting all the other males to get a wife, you get someone with bad breath, ha ha ha," Adi was having a great time. Life can indeed be rather lonely for quite a few of the males. As I was thinking this, a male dragon turned his head slowly and looked into my eyes sadly. There wasn't much I could do to help him, and so we moved on from Komodo Kitchen.

We trekked for an hour in Rinca; crossed a few streams, jumped over big dollops of buffalo dung and saw some guinea fowl, another monogamous creature, busily digging the soil to see what's inside. There is something truly monogamous about Komodo national park. Adi was talking all the while, "I am delighted to have met you because I love people from Singapore. I also love people from China and from India. But I don't like people from Korea and Japan." He went on with his monologue, "I don't like Koreans and Japanese because they would never become friends like we have become." That was not making much sense until he said, "These Koreans and Japanese never paid me any tip." We got the hint and Lobo and I discussed in hushed voices how much more to give him since his fees has already been paid at the park. The forest didn't appear interesting anymore. It was like any tropical jungle, rather monotonous and hot. Stealthily, I kept separately a ten thousand rupiah note to retain Adi's love for Singapore, China and India.

Adi took us to a watering hole where the animals congregated to socialise over a drink. That was also a favourite hunting ground for the dragons but on that day, there were none. As we came back to the kitchen, Adi decided to play the hero. "Go and sit behind that pensioner dragon, I will take some pictures." Later when I saw the pictures, I noticed that I was posing like a shepherd of the Komodos and Lobo was always behind me with a mischievous smile as if she was ready to flee, leaving me behind for a diplomatic chat with the dragons if they ever were to give us a chase. Adi gratified us, "Normally I don't take such pictures. I took it for you only because I love people from Singapore, India and China." I felt sad that Koreans and Japanese had to go back home without any pictures. I gave him the tip in national interest and left Rinca.

Once we got back on Fitra Mandiri, our boat, we saw several small fish surrounding our boat. The father-son pair had already cooked our lunch, simple fare of vegetables and fried fish and some sauce to go along with it. It tasted a little better than the Padang food and we headed for our next stop, a snorkelling point half way between Rinca and Komodo Island. The snorkelling was not very unique and the fish were shyer than the ones we fed in Krabi. Here, they waited for us to release the sweet bread bits and move on before they would devour them. We enjoyed more being on board, watching the hills appear one by one from the sea whose blue was getting stronger with the afternoon sun. By now, Captain Rudy and his son had become more relaxed. Earlier in the morning, both father and son had taken care to erase their existence as much as they could, staying mostly behind the boat's wheel, coming out only to offer us something. But after we invited them to join us for lunch on the boat which they agreed to after much insistence, they opened up.

While I was reading the Lonely Planet, I spotted Captain Rudy's name as a recommended sailor. When I showed that to him, he grinned and wrote down his phone number on a piece of paper, "See, if this is the same number or not." Indeed, indeed, our Captain Rudy was the same as their Captain Rudy. He had come to Flores from Makassar as a sailor and had settled down in Labuan Bajo marrying a local woman. He was a Muslim and at times, I spotted him quietly climbing up on top of the boat's roof to pray. "I have three children," he said, "My eldest daughter can speak English! She has a big job. She works in an expensive hotel in Labuan Bajo." Captain Rudy didn't own the boat and got a share from the whole price, "I want my son to take over from me this business of sailing for tourists." He usually spoke in a rough way to Grishal, his son, and the father and son relationship had seemed transactional of sorts, with Grishal obeying whatever was being said but the tone of his voice showing the hint of a rebel. It was the irony of relationships that while they were individually so warm to us, there seemed to be a cold wall between them. But when we got back on the boat after snorkelling, we did witness a tender moment between them as they stood together and dropped tiny pieces of bread for the fish to eat.

Grishal always looked too serious for his age, but when he smiled, which he started doing more and more, a baby would reveal itself with the cheeks puffing up and the eyes brightening up. He had stopped going to school and knew that he would be doing this probably for the rest of his life.

Sailing seems a lot about tying and untying knots. At the point of reaching shores, Grishal would untie a knot in a thick rope with the anchor to drop it. As we left the shore, he would do the reverse again, tying a knot. When the wind was favourable, the father and son untied a few knots to make a sail out of a huge plastic sheet, and when the wind turned unfavourable, they converted it into a small lump using a few knots. When the water started splashing on-board, Rudy untied and tied a few knots to make a makeshift curtain out of a plastic sheet and did the reverse when things turned dry. Not to mention the various times they tied and untied knots in plastic bags to take out food, store the waste, and various other supplies. What I considered rather absurd as a child was suddenly all clear to me; was there really any other way we could measure distance and speed in sea other than using nautical miles and knots? Another absurdity for me, the mathematical concept of knot theory, that I had struggled with so much during my graduation days, still remained incomprehensible.

Captain Rudy informed us that we were heading for another snorkelling point, in front of Pantai Merah or Red Beach in Komodo Island. When we asked if we could skip another bout of snorkelling, he said, "No, the fish there would be far better than what you have seen yet." At Pantai Merah, the sand appeared more pink than red and the evening sun was emphasising its colour. The pink colour comes from the remains of dead red corals brought to the shore.

The coral garden beneath the sea was splendid with structures looking like giant green fans and tumorous dollops of orange, bright blue nudibranchs moving over them. We came across a big cuttlefish which had a Zen-like expression. It got Lobo rather unsettled and she dragged me away as fast as she could from this nirvana seeker. I felt sad for the corals, it must have been rather uncomfortable to be constantly nibbled on by fish and walked over by slimy nudibranchs. We got back on the boat after clumsily taking off the snorkelling fins which in my opinion were the most unnecessary and inconvenient contraptions ever made by man.

It was very windy and we started feeling cold. Just then, when we were shivering and hugging our towels, a voice came, "*Mau beli Komodo?*" or "Want to buy some Komodos?" We turned and saw a small canoe next to our boat and a man holding out two small komodo statues. We burst out laughing at the implausibility of that moment, a male nymph rising out of the mysterious depths of the seas to sell us souvenirs. Captain Rudy and Grishal laughed out too, and after a momentary startle, the nymph started laughing too. He left, shyly wishing us a happy journey.

As the sun was about to say goodbye, we dropped anchor at a small bay at Komodo Island, about fifty metres from the nearest hill. Three more tourist boats joined us quietly and anchored themselves at a distance. As I sat at the front of the boat, the sense of enormity of the landscape in its entirety started to set in and the sun began distributing its parting gift to mankind, an array of colours in the sky. As for the hills and the sea, their bright green and blue colours gently fell asleep as the sun left after tenderly pulling a giant dark blanket over them. A bunch of flying foxes, which locals call 'Batman' left the hills. I recalled the poem *In the Lodi Gardens* by Octavio Paz:

The black, pensive, dense
Domes of the mausoleums
Suddenly shot birds
Into the unanimous blue

At that beautiful moment, when I was at the verge of being the second man on earth to attain nirvana, loud generators were turned on one by one at all the three boats. As the world was denied yet another messiah and the accompanying religion, Grishal turned on the music system unleashing golden rock chants of *Highway to Hell* and *Sweet Child of Mine*.

Three small canoes were approaching us, a lone rower in each of them. Each of them put a knot around our boat and stabilised their canoes. One offered us beer, another pulled out small wooden statues of komodo dragons while the other asked us if we wanted to buy some fish. When we smiled and declined, they just hung around holding on to our boat and keeping quiet. I asked them their names: Ashi, Edi and Tesh. Two of them climbed on to our boat and sat down in front of me. All three of them kept looking at me quietly. I tried to have a conversation; my Bahasa Indonesia had already shed some rust by then after talking all day to Captain Rudy and Grishal. Lobo came over and sat next to me. Soon I transformed into a translator for Lobo. All of them came from the small village on Komodo Island that had about fifteen hundred people. While this small village had been settled by people from all over Indonesia, most of them traced their roots to convicts exiled to that barren island by the Sultan of neighbouring Bima in Sumbawa Island a few hundred years back. Almost all the villagers lived on fishing and occasionally selling small items to tourists.

In the dim lights, all I could see was their lean frames with white eyes. All three had a habit of speaking in unison reiterating each other's points. "I am twenty, he is thirty three," said two of them. Simultaneously, the other guy said, "I am thirty three, these two are in their twenties." That meant that Ashi and Edi were in their twenties while Tesh was thirty three, my age. "I am already married and I have a daughter," said Edi and Tesh together while Ashi stopped at, "I am already married." We got them thinking when we asked them what they would like their daughters to become when they grew up. Now they were speaking separately. Edi said, "Teacher, or perhaps doctor." Tesh then repeated what Edi said and Ashi kept nodding in agreement. Then Tesh said, "No, no, she should become a police woman," and everyone agreed again. "There is a lot of corruption," said Ashi. "Police keep harassing us," said Edi. They taught me the Bahasa Indonesia word for punch, *pukul*. Ashi said, "That's what the police do to us, *pukul*." Edi joined, "So our daughters should join the police so that no one can *pukul* us." We all agreed amid laughter. Edi then suggested, "Why stop at police woman, why not become the president of Indonesia? Even more *pukul*." More laughter followed. Tesh asked us the exchange rate for Singapore dollar. He said, "Two years back, I was paid by a tourist in Singapore dollars. I sold him two statues. I haven't been able to change the dollars yet. Can you change them... But I didn't bring the dollars with me..." he got lost in his thoughts. Edi asked, "Where all have you been to in Indonesia?" Tesh said, "You must be very rich to be able to come to Flores from so far. I have never been anywhere except Komodo and Labuan Bajo. But I have a friend who has been to Bali." They said together, "Someday I hope to go to Bali and work on speed boats. I want to learn some English there." All along, Ashi kept nodding quietly but vigorously. At times, we just sat quietly, looking at one another.

They knew that we were not going to buy anything but they didn't seem to mind that. Tesh said with an air of authority, pointing his finger at us and then throwing it down, "I liked talking to you two." He said that in a rough way that seemed completely earnest. I loved that moment with them at the boat, complete strangers connected by the fragile thread of my broken Bahasa Indonesia and a much intricate and complicated mesh of threads making strangers want to communicate and know about each other.

Captain Rudy called us to come for dinner and the three villagers declined our invitation to join us. Captain Rudy came over to talk to the villagers and bought three komodo sculptures from them, "Ican sell these in town after marking up by a hundred thousand rupiah." Edi, Tesh and Ashi got back into their canoes and were about to sail away when Edi asked, "Do you have some medicines for fever? My daughter has been sick for the last two days." I gave him some paracetamol with directions but asked him to definitely consult a doctor if things don't improve. Edi agreed to do so but the three spoke together again, "Our village has no doctor. We only have a mosque."

Dinner was deep fried chicken and some haberdashery of vegetables. After dinner, Lobo and I went up the roof of the boat and placed two bed length cushions on top. Our plan was to count a few of the stars. We kept lying for a long time and one by one, each of the three boats turned off their lights and the noisy generators. In every boat, dinner was over and the crew had washed up the dishes. In the darkness that followed, the starlight was still providing silhouette to the hills. What were the Komodo dragons doing over there?

It was a moonless night and distant galaxies were visible as glittering mist. Lobo compared the sky with a dark bowl punctured by several small holes through which the outside world was pouring in. We turned over to look at the sea. The water was rippling gently and we could hear small fish breaking the surface every now and then. And then we noticed the magic of the reflections of two bright stars flirting with each other. In the rippling water, their reflections bounced against each other and then jumped away, stretched their shape and then suddenly shrunk again. These stars, separated by billions of light years for billions of years, got to embrace and play with each other every night in these waters. As we watched this spectacle in utter numbness, we recounted how our own lives had criss-crossed. Once, I had drawn an abject representation of the world map and asked Lobo to use a blue pen and draw a continuous line on it going through the places she had been to as she reached that present moment of her life from her birth. I did the same thing for my life with a red pen. Both of us had been born at small towns in the north-eastern parts of our respective countries. She was born at a village two hours from Shenyang in Liaoning province of China and I was born in Lumding, a town of fifty thousand people in Assam, whose only claim worth anything was that it had a railway junction. The lines we drew had remained steady and very short for a long time and then suddenly burst out to reach in long leaps all the continents, forming a jumble of strings dropped on the floor with some isolated strands spread out. At San Francisco and southern India, our two lines had been together without us knowing. They had then moved on in bursts before heading for a dash to Singapore where it became steady again and now about to finally merge into one another. Along the course, our birth into different religions, our years of upbringing in different cultures, our food habits, belief systems and our divergent preferences in all aspects of life had lost enough of themselves, gained enough of peculiarities and morphed into a mishmash of personalities that had come to accept one another as soul mates. That night, the conditions at Komodo Island were as such. We began self-congratulating ourselves for where we had ended up. It was a night when the romantic hormones in our brains were having an easy win against all other emotions and we felt as one with the stars, the sky, the hills, the sea, what lay deep within the sea, the fish, the Komodos, the boats, Captain Rudy, Grishal, Edi, Tesh, Ashi, and the other tourists and crews enjoying their own fantasies around us.

Then Lobo noticed that things around us were rather wet. There was a lot of humidity in the air and though the weather was quite comfortable, the condensation was making all surfaces very wet. We flipped over the beds and kept dreaming beyond the stars.

Lobo's nose started protesting soon. We headed down where Captain Rudy and Grishal had set up our makeshift beds and themselves gone to sleep. We didn't want to sleep that night, just like we had stayed awake all night a year back on the crater rim of Mount Rinjani. That night, the sky was clear and the moon was full; the solitude of the landscape had enticed us to brave the chilly winds and step out of our tent to catch yet another glimpse of the beauty that surrounded us. But when I had walked a few steps to take a toilet break, I accidentaly stepped on some human excreta, gift from an earlier group of trekkers. The rest of that romantic night, I kept rubbing my shoe on every grass patch around me to get rid of the leftovers of this man with a giant anus.

I woke up early the next day hoping to catch the sunrise for all tourists love sunrise. Captain Rudy was already awake. I went over to the top of the boat and saw a small disturbance in the orange red sea which slowly took the shape of a tiny boat creating a giant V shape on the sea surface with its gentle progress towards us. It was Ashi, the youngest of the three, who had kept quiet for most of the time the night before. He had brought eggs for us, part of the deal between him and Captain Rudy. As Ashi left, he started coughing loudly. The hills coughed back in empathy. He kept on coughing till he became a small dot in the sea and the hills quietened.

After an early breakfast of bread, omelette and bananas, it was time to drop anchor at Komodo Island. Here, we met our park ranger, Affandi. He had lean hollow shoulders and deep furrows in his forehead. He had Obama ears that had been tapping interstellar signals for a long time. The top of his head was as flat as the Table Top Mountain. Some persons are born to look honest and he was undoubtedly one of them. He confirmed, "I don't have any hatred for Japanese or Korean tourists." That morning at Komodo, the short trees along the trail cast long shadows and the weather was cool. I took off my Arab headgear and started whistling. Affandi placed his anti-dragon Y shaped pole on his shoulders and started humming too. Lobo started singing a Chinese song from the Long March period. Affandi told us the same details about Komodo Dragons that we already knew by heart by now. He too was traumatised by the Komodo mother's penchant for devouring their own children. We were in high spirits, so we avoided passing judgement on these mothers.

I asked Affandi about local myths and legends about Komodos. Although I am as extreme an atheist as any non-human animal or plant can be, I am always gullible for myths and legends. Their innocence, simplicity, magic, and surreal nature always make me crave for more. After all, these myths always insist that the evidence of good's persistent victory over evil is all around us. They explain everything without using supercomputers and linear accelerators. They make a man make love to a bird and a bird steal babies from a man. Who wouldn't fall for them? Somehow, while all the details about these myths are vividly remembered, their date of occurrence is inevitably forgotten. All we know is that all myths happened at the same time; a long, long time ago.

I was hoping for some grand myth about Komodos. They seemed capable enough to carry the world on their back like the mythological serpents and tortoises in Indian, Chinese and other mythologies or my favourite Faronika, the mystical fish in Slovenian mythology who, as the word goes, carries the world on its back and will one day dive into the cosmic sea and sink the earth if there is too much evil. But Affandi had a rather tame tale to tell.

"Once upon a time, there was a woman called the Dragon Princess who lived on Komodo and married a man called Najo. Dragon Princess was a complex character and was supposed to have magical powers. One day she laid an egg and hid it in a cave. This made sense, for otherwise, she would surely have been suspected of adultery even by a gullible husband. It turned out that the egg, when hatched, unleashed a baby

Komodo Dragon. Someone gave it the name Ora. Ora became big and strong, biting buffaloes, waiting a week for them to die from the venom, and then munching them in full. Incidentally, Dragon Princess also gave birth to a human baby at the same time as Ora. The boy was named Gerong, who too became big and strong eating chicken and yams. One day, Gerong went hunting and was chasing a deer. Ora too was chasing the same deer. When Gerong saw Ora, he became very angry." This was expected because Komodo Dragons don't look like creatures who would be loved by anyone other than their mothers, and in their case, even their mothers didn't love them, bar as food. Affandi continued, "So Gerong began attacking Ora. Just about when Gerong was about to kill Ora, their mother, the Dragon Princess, appeared and told Gerong about his half-sister. Gerong took pity on Ora and let her recover. They lived happily ever after." Of course, no one questioned Dragon Princess about her dubious pregnancy. "That's why people on this island to this day don't mind the dragons and till recently, used to feed them once a year with deer meat before the practice was banned by the government," Affandi concluded in his baritone.

In one part of the jungle, there was a barren patch covered with dry leaves and there we found two huge Komodos holding on to the earth in their typical style. Affandi took the customary pictures of us behind the dragons in the same style as the guide had done at Rinca. Probably, the training for park rangers included taking pictures of tourists behind Komodos. The two Komodos had excreted a lot of white matter around them. "The white colour in the faeces comes from the calcium in the bones of prey they eat because Komodos are unable to absorb this calcium," explained Affandi. I didn't know the right words in Bahasa

Indonesia to ask Affandi if the Komodos suffered from osteoporosis because of that.

The paws of the Komodos looked vile enough with long aquiline claws. Back in Singapore, a sales agent from some evangelical Christian sect had once approached us with a great pitch, "Why did God give us gaps in between our fingers? So that someone special comes and fills those gaps by holding your hand forever." Lobo had asked her why God wanted to keep ducks lonely. Over here, the Komodos seemed lonely despite the cherished divine gift of finger gaps.

After saying goodbye to them, we began climbing a grass-carpeted hill and after a short trek, we were at its peak. Right in front of us, behind the slopes, was a great forest. Beyond them lay the jagged peaks of Komodo Island carving out the sea. There were many white cockatoos in the forest. They would suddenly create a lot of noise and then stay quiet for a long time. Sometimes they would fly in droves only to come back to their original place after a few minutes. Just ten metres from us, we spotted a small Komodo dragon, probably a female. This one had climbed all the way up and looked rather awkward and hesitant. We saw a big dump of white granular faeces or *'kotoran'* next to it. No wonder, it felt shy to be caught in the act. We tried to take a few pictures of her against the panorama of the blue sky, the peaks, the forest and the sea, but no angle could capture what we could see. Both Lobo and I felt disappointed with the entire camera making industry. They spent millions on flashy advertisements in glossy magazines but at best, they could only partially replicate what the eyes can see.

On our way back, Affandi spotted two flying lizards. He had mentioned them before and I had then had a strong urge to see one. The flying lizards are rather tiny, as long as a finger. Their body colouration is well camouflaged against tree trunks which they love to hug but their wings once spread, can be colourful and flashy. The ones we spotted had small yellow spots spread radially from their base behind the front legs. It took an expert eye to spot them and Affandi caught each one easily by the tail. Although these Chihuahuas of the lizard kingdom can fly or rather jump and glide; when grounded, they are slow with lazy instincts. No wonder baby Komodos make a feast of them. Affandi hung the two by their tails and both struggled for a while before becoming still. Then suddenly they spread their wings, keeping their bodies still. It was as if they were saying, "Ok, this is what you people love to see. Then see, here are our wings. See as much as you want and then let us go. Alright, come on, that's enough, now let us go." Affandi couldn't hear them talk and gave them to Lobo to hold. After the expected screaming, Lobo placed one on my nose while holding on to its tail. Its tiny claws felt like small pins. Soon it began scratching my nose and it was my turn to scream. Overjoyed at this cherished encounter, we let them go. We gave Affandi a reasonable tip, more than what we gave to our Japan-Korea bashing, India-Singapore-China loving Adi.

On our way back, we spotted a lonely black dolphin taking dips in the choppy sea. We said farewell to Captain Rudy and Grishal. We had loved them for their humility and politeness. Even though we were having a business transaction, they had genuinely wanted us to be comfortable and enjoy the trip, always having an unobtrusive eye for what we might need, where they might be of help, simple gestures like running to provide a pillow at the slightest hint that we were planning to lie down. I wondered if our paths will cross again. Will Captain Rudy make a decent margin on the wooden komodo statues? Will Grishal become Captain Grishal? Will Captain Rudy's English speaking daughter help him to finally own his boat?

Labuan Bajo was hot as expected and I got back into my costume. We waited at Louis' shop and the van to take us to Ruteng came on the dot. Out of it came the Brazilian soccer star Ronaldo, before he had become fat and had been trapped with transvestites. Out here, he was driving the van. The van quickly climbed up from Labuan Bajo and kept climbing and climbing. Cool breezes seeped in through the windows. We were on the mountains of Flores.

Ruteng, My Ruteng

Rrutengg, that's how locals call the place. The travel guides don't allow the place a lot of glamour, just honouring it as a stopover along the journey from Labuan Bajo to the more illustrious town of Bajawa. One tourist had described the place in internet forums as the dirtiest town in Indonesia and had posted pictures of garbage heaps on the internet. So we had come with low expectations. Ruteng would be just a stop to plan the next leg of our journey.

But in spite of everything, something always works for a tropical hill town. The escape from the heat of Labuan Bajo as we climbed towards Ruteng was already refreshing our souls. We were travelling along the famed Trans Flores Highway that lies on Flores like a giant lazy serpent trying to fit in somehow in a small narrow box and sleep. Seven hundred kilometres of a serpent fitted within an island three hundred kilometres long; so it zigzags between north and south, climbs up over a thousand metres only to get wet by the sea after a little while and then climb up again. One of its two heads is at Labuan Bajo and the other at Maumere, from where it waits to swallow humans dropping off at the ferry terminals. Over the next few days, we would spend a lot of time with the serpent, riding her slippery back. And lo and behold, there was the caterpillar stretching comfortably over Ronaldo's dashboard with its twinkly eyes and soft padded legs.

The road from Labuan Bajo to Ruteng winds around the tropical hills, closely watched over by patches of bamboo trees. We twisted our necks in unbelievable positions to catch glimpses of the sunset over the hills.

We were sitting next to a young tax officer, Pedor. He had been shy and quiet initially but after I tried my Bahasa Indonesia with him, he morphed into the garrulous Fidel Castro. All I could do was to just look at him and keep nodding as he told me one thing or the other, mostly to do with the attractions in Flores. He offered us food he was carrying for himself and started showing me pictures and videos of his family. He had a young son who was yet to start talking. Pedor was beaming with pride, "He is so intelligent, see, see..." He kept showing me on his phone long videos of his son trying to do things like pulling a cloth around the house or throwing a doll and then picking it up again. Good old Christopher Hitchens had once written that a mother talking about her children is the most boring and humourless thing on earth. A father talking about his children probably isn't too far behind. I made a big mistake in adopting an approving body language for the first few minutes as if a toddler managing to keep himself busy was showing all signs of being able to rival Einstein or Willie Sutton, the infamous bank robber. I was hoping for a way to escape from this 'Hell is other's babies.' The serenity with which Lobo was enjoying the views from the car window was annoying me even more. I took inspiration from Willie Sutton and pretended to be suffering from altitude sickness, car sickness, motion sickness, headache and indigestion. Lobo immediately offered to swap seats and there I was, far from the madding child videos. Pedor became quiet, unsure of Lobo's Bahasa Indonesia, and unsure of the propriety of taking to her while I was around. Oh, it is so nice to have good manners still alive in this world.

I stuck my neck out of the van window and in the refreshing breeze, became nostalgic about the pleasures of travelling alone. For the last two years I have been travelling with Lobo and out of male chivalry, I always had to give away the window seat if it was a bus and the aisle seat if it was a plane. The heavier bag would always rest on my tender shoulders and the wrappers and empty plastic bags would always find a home in my pockets. I have raised these pertinent issues and she would always retort that because we travel together, there is always someone to remind me to wash my hands before eating, someone to remind me to always drink hot water to avoid losing my hair, and someone to make sure that all healthy life-enhancing practices are followed, not to mention cheaper costs per person because of sharing. She had as many reasons in favour as I had against to make sure I would always keep feeling nostalgic about those old days of solitude and at the same time never feel like travelling alone again. Nonetheless, from now on, my life had become one of those middle-seat lives.

As we went along the Trans Flores highway, the mountains gave way to green valleys, highland rice fields, big crowds watching an evening soccer match at the school fields, cows returning home disobeying traffic rules, men squatting along the roadside after their day's work, and kids playing badminton over volleyball nets. It was dark when we finally reached Ruteng and as we got down, everyone from the bus wished us a good stay. It felt as if all the other passengers were just waiting for this moment to be able to interact with us in some way. Hearts warmed in the cold night and we set out in the broad lonely streets of Ruteng to find a place to stay.

Ruteng is the capital of Manggarai Regency with a population of over thirty five thousand, mostly Roman Catholic. At an altitude of one thousand two hundred metres, Ruteng had gained worldwide fame once when a cave near the town yielded human-like bones that led to controversy on a Cambrian scale. The discoverers had claimed that the bones belonged to members of a hitherto undiscovered species related to humans and called them Homo Floresiensis. This was based on their distinctive characteristics of small body and brain, features that gave a more common name to the species, 'Hobbit'. The discoverers deduced that these ancestors did use stone tools and may have lived simultaneously alongside modern humans in the island before dying out, about ten to fifteen thousand years ago, a tantalising proposition for many. But the opponents of this theory had instead argued that the bones merely belonged to humans who had pathological defects and therefore died with the small body structure. The final word is yet to be cast on this issue and researchers are hoping to extract genetic material from the bones to obtain conclusive evidence. But so far, the story of the main actors involved had been nothing short of a telenovella. Teuku Jacob, the giant of Indonesian anthropology, had always denounced the claim of the bones being evidence of a new species. However, he had once taken the bones away for his own research without proper permissions and returned them badly damaged with some bones missing. Jacob claimed this was due to a transport mishap while his detractors blamed him for self-delusion, greed and irresponsibility. The Indonesian government then closed off the cave from where the bones were unearthed which was cited by some as a blatant strategy to protect the reputation of Jacob, a national hero. The caves were reopened only after his death in 2007. Such fights and behind the back bitching are inevitable in palaeontology that after all tries to deduce whether flight came before jumping or jumping came before flight on the basis of a small bend in the ankle bone.

The night was chilly and we headed straight for the Kongregasi Santa Maria, a nun's hostel which also accommodated guests at market rates. The place was highly recommended over the internet and even by Louis of Labuan Bajo as the only place worth staying in Ruteng. Their key selling point was a free flow of hot water. Once there, a stern looking nun came out and told us that no rooms were available. The first thought that came was, ok, a few days without hot water, so what. We walked up to the nearby Rima Hotel that claimed to be inspired by Swiss Chalets. It was like a typical Flores hotel, lights dimmer than a star's twinkle, twin beds with soft soggy mattresses, stained walls and floors with evidence of cockroach high-living everywhere. We ran out of Rima but didn't know where else we could find a place to stay for the night. We planned to walk around the main roads and took a break along the roadside to put on warm clothes for the long walk ahead. A shop was open on the other side and two young men from inside called us in. We asked them for nearby hotels, a question that seemed to have stunned them. Looking completely stupefied, one man suggested, "Right!" while the other suggested, "Left!" Both kept on trying to convince us why we should consider only their advice. And then suddenly and simultaneously, they dropped their own convictions to support the other's idea. So now the guy initially saying left was suggesting right and vice versa. To ease their confusion, we took things in our control and I got a map of the town out of my backpack. Once we figured out it was 'left', we explained the directions to both of them. Delighted, they bade us farewell, hoping to see us again.

We walked along and found a ramshackle Masakan Padang restaurant where Lobo wanted to take a toilet break. The mama of the restaurant showed her a hole in the ground that was actually a staircase to the basement where the family lived. A white cat jumped ahead and guided Lobo to the toilet downstairs and then came up to ask me for a tip. It reminded me of the barbecue cat that resided without an address in our condominium complex in Singapore. It would turn up for every barbecue party that happened in the pits by the swimming pool. Sometimes I had even spotted it near the pit booking office hoping to go through the booking dates. The shameless animal would nonetheless pay scant regard for good manners. Whenever it would have to go along a straight line, it would always take a zagged criss-crossed path, forcing tender superstitious hearts to reconsider their journeys.

We checked two more hotels and all were grimmer than what we could tolerate. At one place, not finding anyone at the reception, we walked in, only to find ecstatic moans from inside one room. There seemed to be one man and a few women. Outside the room, there were many statues of Jesus in all sizes with lit candles at their feet. Unsure of what form of ecstasy was being unleashed behind the door; we ran away, our backs bent from the backpack load which seemed to be supporting the whole sky by now. Now our only hope was Losmen Agung, described in a guide book as a basic place by rice fields, a bit far from the city centre. I always have orgasms at the thought of rice fields and had been secretly hoping that we end up staying at this place.

As we headed towards Agung, the road became empty, the shops around were closed and the street lights were off. Guided by the moonlight, we knocked at a wrong place which looked like an abandoned small palace. A guard came out, his face fully covered with a blanket. Two huge barking dogs followed him. He told us to go further.

The houses along the road were getting sparse and we could hear the rumbling of a stream getting louder and louder.

The premises of Losmen Agung had a huge gate and in the yard by the side, many discarded small trucks were meditating. In front of what seemed like a lobby, there was a giant water truck. We entered a huge circular hall. Two people, fully covered in blankets were watching TV. There was a broad staircase leading up to the second floor. The sparse furniture looked very old. The walls looked grimy and in need of some dusting. The whole place looked very similar to how haunted bungalows are shown in Indian movies.

We fidgeted in the hall not knowing what to do because no one approached us. When I asked one of the two people watching TV if the place had rooms available, he slowly moved his blanket to reveal his mouth and just smiled. The other guy slowly revealed his face too. They had typical features of highland people. Both discussed something and then kept staring at the TV set. When I asked again, the first one got out of his blanket and reluctantly walked out. While he was away, we watched TV with the older man; it was the news. After a while, the young man came back with another person. When he saw us, he came up to us running and once he reached us, suddenly crossed his arms in front and nodded; the time old gesture to indicate humility and servitude in some way. He looked like a Pakistani, sharp features, straight hair, fair skin, and a pointed nose. His name was Adi. He said that many rooms were available and took us upstairs to show a room. This further raised my suspicions about the place being haunted because only haunted hotels always have many available rooms.

The room was huge with the same dim lights, stained walls, and dirty flooring. There was a back door which I went to open and Adi rushed up to me to keep it closed. Surely this place was haunted; but I kept quiet. I asked Adi about breakfast and he said they didn't provide any. Which haunted hotel ever bothered with breakfasts? However, the mattresses were firm and Lobo decided to take up the place immediately. In a flash, Adi gave us the keys and disappeared. He didn't take any details or any deposit from us; either the place was very honest or it was just purely haunted.

After Adi left, I went back to the back door and opened it. There was a small balcony without railings connecting all the rooms. It was facing the graveyard of the trucks. The balcony was very dirty and wet; exposed iron bars were jutting out from the cracks. Back inside, I found Lobo overjoyed to see a basin opposite the bathroom door. She opened the tap and the water fell straight down the basin sink hole on the floor because the drainage pipe had been removed. On the bed, I spotted fresh stains of blood. And just then, the back door opened with the familiar creaking sound and a strong gust of wind came in. The ghost was probably an Indian or some local who had seen a lot of Indian horror movies. I was too tired to greet her with fear and crashed, hoping she would keep herself busy with her night to night tasks.

The next morning, everything was delightful and we were still alive without much apparent blood loss. The air was crisp and cool. In the lush green graveyard for trucks, the dark shapes were now replaced by jauntily painted vans whose insides had been claimed over by feminine vines with lovely pink flowers. Further down, the rice fields climbed up to deep green hills holding up a magic blue sky. Adi came by and surprise, surprise, gave us some breakfast, sweet bread and coffee. Delighted, we tried our luck and asked if he could arrange for hot water. He nodded and ran away. We must have been nice to the ghosts the night before.

Downstairs, the two men were still watching TV. They seemed delighted to see us alive and gave us loud greetings, quite unlike their ways the previous night. Adi came back running, somehow managing to drag a plastic oil barrel filled with steaming water. Like a well-mannered puppy, he waited a flash second to cross his hands to receive our thank you as an appreciation, and then ran away again. Suddenly, I realized that there was something good in the air about Ruteng.

We headed for the spider rice fields of Cara village, about twenty minutes from Ruteng. The bus terminal was at the end of the town and at the town gates, there were two sculpted statues, one at each pillar of the gate, of a man and woman greeting visitors with folded hands. Their expressions suggested that they were in a lot of pain, either very scared of the visitors or they know that some great misfortune was about to fall on their town soon. Such statues can be found all over Flores and usually they all have the same expression. Another favourite place for statues is the schools. With big scary eyes, the statues of young students in front of the schools look eerie, especially after school hours when the complexes are deserted. Occasionally, they display communist style strong movements, legs marching in sync, girl and boy, jointly holding a flame high above that looks more like an ice-cream cone.

Cara is a small village, ten minutes' walk from a larger village, Cancar, where the buses from Ruteng to Labuan Bajo make a quick stop along the Trans Flores highway. Where the bus and the caterpillar dropped us, there was a toddler waiting for us. He was yet to learn how to talk but managed to call his master, another young boy, probably eight or nine years old. Led by our young guides, we walked up the hill, a path lined by tall grasses. At the top, the village was empty because most would have gone working in the fields. After waiting for a while, a lady came out and asked us to sign a guestbook. We were expecting this, a well honoured tradition in Flores and Sumba where if you visit a village, you are expected to sign a guestbook and make a small donation. It may not exactly conform to universal ideas of hospitality but can be tolerated with the understanding that the extremely poor people living in these villages have limited ways of benefiting from tourism. After this ritual, the kids took us to the viewing point where a large panorama opened up. In the valley down below were large circular patterns of rice fields, radially spreading out from their respective centres. Small shapes of people could be seen bent over, busy with the rice plants, orange brown as they were ready for harvest. Steep dark green hills guarded this valley.

The spider web pattern of the rice fields is an outcome of the land distribution practices of the Manggarai people. The village head distributes land among the villagers in parcels of triangular patterns or Lodok, starting at the centre, like pizza cuts, which from top looks like a series of concentric circles cut into equal segments by lines radiating out from the centre.

Our young guides were rather quiet when compared to children we had met before. They looked grumpy and when we gave them stickers, they took them without smiling. We followed them down and the older of the two whispered, "Money." After settling him for his service, we started walking to Cancar to get our caterpillar ride to Ruteng. A very old man saw us and suddenly gained the energy of a sprinter to rush up to us and asked, "Money." We continued walking without talking to each other. Something had disturbed us. As for me, I had always been the biggest advocate for Indonesian hospitality and had told Lobo a lot about how the so called happiest nation on earth warms up to strangers without expecting anything. Probably Lobo understood what I was thinking and made my situation lighter with her silence.

The town of Cancar was only a five minute walk from Cara. Its claim to township lay in the fact that it had a small market and a junction where bemos would stop on their way to bigger towns. We came across many young students walking along the road as the local school had just closed for the day. We created a bustle among them. Among the older students, the girls started harassing the boys, "Talk to them in English." As they pushed the boys towards us, the boys became very shy, put their head down, started scratching the back of their heads and attempted a few words, "Good morning, How are you, Where you from?" Every attempt was ridiculed with lots of laughter from the girls. Wishing us a happy stay they moved on, laughing and teasing each other. Then we came across a younger bunch of students, probably in the primary school. They tried to do the same thing as the older students, just that the roles had reversed. The boys were pushing the girls towards us, "Talk to them in English." We gave each one of them stickers of butterflies and flags of countries which they immediately pasted on their notebooks and bags with a lot of delight.

We came across a man making a cock dance by turning his hand round and round above its head. The cock, like a cumbersome ballerina, turned and turned. We stopped by a small restaurant where a toddler kept telling us, "I have already had shower."

We took a bemo back to Ruteng with a pig tied on the roof. With big fat lips, slightly open, he almost looked like laughing and enjoying the balmy morning. Perhaps, he was being taken to the slaughterhouse. In the van behind us, someone had placed a wet t-shirt in the front for drying, kept in place by the window wiper. All along the road, people had put clothes for drying on top of manicured hedges. It appeared as if people here preferred to build fences out of washed clothes.

Back in Ruteng, we drove past beautiful rice fields, some lime green, some bright orange, flanked by the now familiar green hills. There was a lot of commotion as the driver and a few others tried to get the pig back on earth. It started screaming and throwing its limbs around like a grumpy baby. A naked toddler travelling with one of the passengers got even more disturbed and started wailing loudly. This made the pig go quiet. We offered the baby stickers and he threw them away. One old lady offered him a candy and it also got the same handling. After the father hugged him closely to the chest, he calmed down and fell asleep. It was indeed a slaughterhouse.

Ruteng is primarily Catholic and the shrine of Virgin Mary on top of the hill, Golo Curu, attracts people from around the region. Children surrounded us all along the way. First a big group of young boys wanted to show us a small bird they had caught. When we asked them for a picture along with them, they became very shy and started pushing each other to the front of the photo line. Further up, a bunch of young girls were more sober. Very gracefully, they took our stickers and then posed with modest smiles for a picture.

As we climbed on, we began seeing the true beauty of Ruteng. Patches of colour were everywhere. Green fields of mustard with yellow button like flowers had proud cocks walking in between them. Gardens full of red leaved trees were looking over tidy houses with red tiled roofs. The houses came in all shades of bright happy colours, lime green, sky blue, lime yellow and an occasional orange.

The winding road to the top soon got lonely, lined with tombs with red tiles and a series of gaudily coloured small cement statues cut along the hillside showing events linked to Jesus carrying his cross. The overbearingly sorrowful expressions in those statues were in stark contrast to the joyous nature that was all around.

The altar at the top was solemn. There were a few young people who had come to enjoy the views and the company of their loved one. Facing away from the altar, they were sitting on top of the wall that formed the boundary between the cliffs and the shrine's grounds. Stretched below and spread out over miles were terraces of rice fields, in brown and green hues. The trees on the slopes around the shrine were covered with thick vines that spurted out an abundance of violet flowers.

A young man with long open hair was moving from one group of people, talking to each one of them. He had a handsome face with lean features that revealed a life of physical hardship. His long flowing hair was kept back using a band. He was probably in his late thirties. His name was Hendrik. Hendrik could speak in broken English. "I come on my motorbike to this shrine often. It's a two-hour journey from my hometown. But I like talking to other people who come here and to know more about them," he said. "I once lived in Bali and worked in a hotel. I learnt English there. Out in Bali, I used to drink a lot and enjoy life. Then one day I decided that I had had enough enjoy and went to Jakarta to find some other work." My scandal-hungry mind deduced that possibly, in Bali, he was working as a Kuta cowboy, ferrying around foreign lovelorn women across roads and life. Hendrik continued, "In Jakarta, I found a job as a welder and met many people from Flores who were also working as welders there. Together, we built many bridges all around Java. One day, I asked myself why are there no good welders in Flores? Why can't Flores have good bridges? So I came back and started my shop. I have a small welding shop. My welding is very good. It can easily pass anyone's quality control." He looked happy, gentle and extremely courteous. Welding had taken the Kuta cowboy out of him.

The faces of Ruteng are a curious mix. Some looked straight out of Brazil while some would have been quite at home among the Rastafaris of Jamaica. Men came in sizes between four feet to six feet. Noses spread from razor sharp to elephant's feet. Hair diverged from slippery straight to electric heater curls. And skin colour merged from shiny black to albino white. Ruteng is a United Nations of human faces.

We took a bemo to Kampung Ruteng, a traditional village near the town. Every driver and his sidekick in the bemos have a daredevil attitude; loud music blaring from high pitched audios, rows of small circular mirrors hanging in front, playboy bunny stickers pasted all over, and quirky quotes and images decorating the windows. On one window, there was the caricature of a spiky haired man kissing a nun. On another, was written in huge cartoon fonts, "Free Love, Boom".

The sidekick of our bemo's driver, less than five feet tall, decided to join us for the tour of Kampung Ruteng. I was sure he would grow up to look like the Brazilian soccer star Ronaldo but he told me, "I am a grown up already, I am seventeen. Manggarai people can be small in size but big in age." He seemed far from the world of familiar teenage obsessions and was very nervous with our camera when we asked him to take pictures. All along, he kept looking at us as if we were crazy aliens discarded from the mothership. Perhaps he couldn't make any sense of why we were so excited to see a cow knotted to a small tree with a bright pink nose ring or why we came all the way only to distribute small stickers to children. I felt happy to have him around. I felt like placing him in a different context like Singapore and watch him as he navigated through its charms.

By now, Ruteng had already warmed our hearts. Being a transit town, people here were not used to seeing foreigners during the day. As such, curious stares with half-smiles filled in all the spaces we walked by and if we took a pause to go and talk to anyone, the half-smile would turn into outright grinning delight. Somehow, all such people would assume that we were in need of help. When we paused in front of a street vendor selling sweet pancakes, passers-by surrounded us to offer advice, "Try the chocoloate flavour. That's the best. Eat it fast and then get one more." When we dropped by a fruit seller to buy some bananas, another group assembled to advise the seller, "Give them that bundle, no that one, yes, this is the best." When we approached a mobile handset store to ask for help regarding registering the local sim card I had bought in Bali, the entire shop converged and volunteered, "Put in my address for the registration! Please put in mine." When we went to the only supermarket in town, we were surrounded by all their staff offering us help. Some went to the point of bringing items to our hands if our body exhibited the faintest incline towards the direction of that item. The only cold place in Ruteng was the Kongregasi Santa Maria where we had been firmly denied accommodation in a tourist-starved town. Perhaps, the nuns had been wary of us. A young couple, from different races, was surely a recipe for devil's nightly brew.

Even Losmen Agung had turned into a friendly and literally warm haunted house. Earlier, Adi had provided Lobo with four thick blankets and was willing to provide more. Lobo, who can never have enough blankets, was delighted at this prospect of an endless supply of blankets. The two people we had seen the day before when we first got inside Agung, were still there, in exactly the same manner. They seemed to have an insatiable appetite for television news. Seeing Lobo sneeze a few times, they suddenly became very active and got out of their television-watching hibernation. The older of the two got us a traditional oil to rub on the back while the younger one searched for Adi to serve us a big flask of warm water and some hot tea. Some of the other guests joined in and began to offer their expert advice on how to deal with a cold. They were all drivers of cargo trucks, taking a break along their journeys back and forward on the Trans Flores Highway. Losmen Agung was their favourite haunt because it was cheap and had a huge parking lot. We shared fruits with them and they gave us biscuits and prawn crackers.

It was then time for chess and that kept all engrossed for hours. The lead players were one old driver with a big moustache and the older one of the news loving couple. The rest including ourselves divided into two groups supporting one of the two, some kneeling around them and some overlooking their shoulders. We kept sinking them in a torrent of advice. Eventually, the driver was at the verge of winning. After every move that further shackled his opponent, he would unleash a jaunty, "Oh, Oh, Oh!" Finally, with no escape route left, the losing player scattered all the pieces with a broad sweep of his hand and a big laugh.

From time to time, we could see Adi pass by in his swift half run. He always appeared to be busy yet missing; but somehow he knew when anyone needed him. Only at night, I found him settled at one place, on top of the water tank, in the dark and chilly night, trying to repair the pump that had stopped working. When we finally left Ruteng, we had offered him fifty thousand rupiah or five dollars for all the services he had provided. He was shocked at why we were doing so. After a few moments of hesitation, he understood, took the money, and again crossed his arms in front, waiting for our next command.

While the eagerness of Ruteng people to help was endearing, sometimes the unwarranted help could come at an inopportune moment. As we took a stroll around the streets of Ruteng during the evening, the tilted sunlight and clear skies had saturated the colours of the entire landscape. The sky was bluer, rooftops more orange, and the carpeted hills more tinted. Small soft lumps of white cloud were idling over these hills, a sight that took Lobo to an emotional high. Having grown up in the tropical highlands of Assam, such sights were rather familiar to me. But Lobo, a creature of the flatlands of Liaoning, had a strong yearning for misty mountains that have been millennially romanticized in Chinese literature and the arts. She described the setting as her magical moment and before she could finish the outpouring of her stream of consciousness, there was a loud "Hello friend" from a group of young boys. They ran up to us and started talking. The smart Joe of the group was another Adi, "I want to practice my English with you." After the initial introductions, he offered to take us to our next destination, Wae Rebo. "I don't have any means of transport. I am just a student," he said, "But I can surely arrange for something." Upon asking, he added, "I don't know the way to Wae Rebo but I can ask around tonight." Upon further asking, he went on, "I don't know much about the culture of the place but we can know once we get there." He wouldn't charge us anything for his own time and just wanted to enjoy our precious company. Lobo's magical moment was disappearing with the setting sun and I saw that she had quietly walked a few steps away from us leaving me alone to indulge in Adi's English training. After convincing Adi that we were still undecided about going to Wae Rebo and so couldn't confirm with him, we left hurriedly taking down the phone number of someone he knew.

Cold weather makes one feel hungrier. A friend had once come up with an ingenious way to lose calories and stay fit, by just drinking tons upon tons of cold water. His logic was that the body would seek to raise the temperature of water to thirty seven degree Celsius, the normal body temperature, and therefore to burn five hundred calories, equivalent to a seven to eight kilometre run for a seventy kilo person, he would just need to drink eighteen litres of water every day. He would also carry ten one-litre empty bottles with him to store the urine he would be passing as a result of this. I never saw him actually do this for real but he was a rather lean man who never indulged in much physical activity. But in Ruteng, his logic was indeed working and more often than not we were always looking for food. But this is where, even Ruteng, the town that we later marketed to everyone as a better deal on earth than even our hometowns, couldn't escape from the Masakan Padang stranglehold. As the Italian communist theoretician Antonio Gramsci would put it, this was cultural hegemony at its best. Because everyone eats Masakan Padang, they only know Masakan Padang, and they only eat Masakan Padang, and they only serve Masakan Padang. In this deep fried ocean, there were scatterings of a few *bakso* or beef ball soup stalls. Outside the supermarket, there was also a small cart selling pau or steamed lumps of rice paste with chicken or sweet fillings inside. This was very popular since the owner was the only pau seller for many miles and his cart had become a sweet spot for romance as many young couples floated around it to renew their vows, each one holding a giant white pau.

After consulting our newest friends at Losmen Agung, we headed out for the strongly recommended Titin's place. It was a shop selling three kinds of soups, chicken, beef and goat. The walls were grimy but the place seemed to be popular with young men who came in groups. The soup counter was manned by two muscular young ladies. At Titin's palace, Ibu Titin was everywhere. Every soup had the prefix Titin's added to it, Titin's chicken soup, Titin's goat soup, and even Titin's orange juice. The table cloths were nothing more than transparent plastic sheets over several copies of the menu, Ibu Titin shouting out of them. Large posters of the Titin menu were all over the walls. We met Ibu Titin only at the time of checking out. We were expecting a hollering big mama but she turned out to be a slender four feet tall lady, probably in her mid-thirties. With her gentle smile, she seemed almost hesitant to take the money from us. We were satisfied that it was not another meal of Masakan Padang. But we were still craving for vegetables. When we had visited the crowded Ruteng pasar or market, it was overflowing with vegetables of all kinds. Where did all those vegetables disappear? Unless people bought them only to dispose of them immediately at the infamous garbage dumps which had been mentioned by one of the travellers who had written about Ruteng on the internet as the dirtiest town on earth. Alas, we couldn't find those garbage dumps. We set our hope for vegetables on the village of Wae Rebo, our next destination. But we were glad that we would come back to Ruteng, and stay at Losmen Agung, where the friendly ghosts played chess.

Back to basics, back to Wae Rebo

Wae Rebo has had a curious reversal of fortunes. An isolated traditional village; initially it was only visited by the genuinely off-the-beaten-track foreign tourists. But of late, the village had gained some reputation and respect within Indonesia and many local tourists visited the village. Consequently, it increasingly fell off the radar for foreign tourists and was not even mentioned in some of the more popular guide books about the region. However, when it comes to tourism in Indonesia, and particularly in places other than Bali; words such as many and numerous need to be perceived within a certain context. Even in the most well-known attraction of Flores, the coloured lakes of Kelimutu, it is perfectly possible to be the only visitor even during peak season. So in the case of Wae Rebo, many tourist arrivals meant that there was at least one arrival every month. When we checked the guestbook at Wae Rebo, the last visitor had come a month back.

Nonetheless, everyone at Ruteng knew about Wae Rebo and seemed to respect our intent to visit the place. Many said they would have loved to join us for the trip. On a few bemos, we saw in big prints, "Back to basics, back to Wae Rebo". For the Manggarai people who lived in Flores, a trip to Wae Rebo was some sort of a cultural pilgrimage, to experience their ancient *adat* or customs. The people of Wae Rebo also welcomed them with open arms, providing lodging to any visitor from the Manggarai tribe, without any monetary expectations. For us, the place seemed remote and mythical enough to consider the trip, and so we headed to the misty mountains, in whose laps slept Wae Rebo.

We were going with two brothers, Emyl and Sil, on their motorbikes. Emyl, the older of the two was a short man, around four feet five inches, with South Asian features. His face looked very kind and his deep voice was rather comforting. Sil, younger than Emyl by ten years, looked fashionable with his cropped hair and leather jackets. He had a hint of youthful arrogance in him. Both were hanging around the motorbike or *ojek* stand near the Ruteng pasar. When we went looking for one, they were the first to approach us. They agreed to take us to Wae Rebo for four hundred thousand rupiah or about forty five American dollars. It was a two-day journey and they volunteered to stay with us at Wae Rebo. The brothers had seemed to be lacking in the usual street-smart attitude of the ojek drivers. And slowly as we progressed with our journey, the two became part of our group instead of being indifferent service providers. Emyl, the eldest among us, soon assumed the role of the leader and interlocutor for our group.

The journey truly mattered as much as the destination or even more when we headed for Wae Rebo. It was only fifty kilometres from Ruteng on the map. But we had to accept in disbelief when Emyl and Sil told us that it would take at least four hours of driving followed by another four hours of hiking through deeply forested hills. But this was East Indonesia where distances were best expressed in hours and days rather than metres or kilometres. And journey times strangely congregated around the same mark, four hours. It took four hours to travel from Labuan Bajo to Ruteng, a distance of one hundred and forty kilometres by road. It also took four hours to travel from Ruteng to Bajawa. And so it was if one wanted to go from Bajawa to Ende, or from Ende to Maumere, and for that matter, from Maumere to Larantuka. It was as if the people of Flores had long ago anticipated

Henry Ford and his crazy wheel machine and set-up their major towns in such a way that they were always four hours from one another. So there was little we could argue about when we got to know that it was going to be another two sets of four hours.

We were out of Ruteng within minutes, heading south towards the Indian Ocean. The town ended abruptly and we climbed up for a while, our path lined by a phalanx of lime green trees with large soft leaves sent in by their generals, the dark green hills behind. At the highest point of the road, there was a sizeable gathering of young couples on motorbikes, having their own private romance in the company of strangers. Emyl and Sil used this point for their toilet break and edged me on to do so as well. I got nervous of being seen by a neatly camouflaged couple and quickly did my deed and ran. After this lover's pinnacle, the road began rolling down to the sea which was now visible in the distance, barely distinguishable from the skies. And floating in between the sky and the ocean was the tiny island of Pulau Mules. The grass-carpeted island, devoid of any trees, got closer and closer to us, all along the journey. It appeared arid, just like Rinca and Komodo. Perhaps the island of Flores was the eldest queen of all the islands in NTT, drawing out all the rain from the surrounding seas and keeping it only for herself, decorating herself in flowery meadows and bamboo kamarbands, while the lesser queens around burnt in envy. As we came down, the rice fields followed the stairs down the hills, their beauty hiding the arduous life of the peasants who were working in the fierce sun.

After two hours of riding through the rice fields, we met the seas, only to start climbing again. Layers were forming in front of us. Young rice fields in green overlooked the mature rice fields in yellow which supported the blue mirror of a sea guarded by the deep green hills and the blue mountains further beyond needling the cloudless skies above while the floating island of Pulau Mules fiddled with the idea of coming closer to us. We passed over one of the better known bridges in Flores, the Wae Mesa, putting its two metal legs over a shallow rocky river. After Wae Mesa, the road turned treacherous and Emyl and Sil struggled to paddle their motorbikes over its heavily pimpled skin. We started coming down again and raced along a long narrow road guarding the hills from the rough seas. Fishing villages with less than a dozen houses each, inhabited by the minority Muslims, were scattered along the narrow rocky coastline. On one isolated rock, a goat was standing, looking out over the ocean into infinity. The air was hot and damp. The chill of Ruteng was far behind in our memories.

After five hours of riding, we reached Dintor, a small fishing town that was the centre of activity for the entire region in that part of the globe. From Dintor, we started climbing again to reach the end of the road, a village called Denge. The air was already cold by now. Lobo was ecstatic from what the six-hour long journey had to offer. That was the delight of travelling by motorbike instead of a car for our eyes could roll over without being limited by what a small window could allow. Smiling, we got down with our sore backs and took off our damp helmets, known in Bahasa Indonesia as another lovely word, *Helem*.

Along the journey, we raced past several small villages. The houses, the shops, the trees and the landscape; they appeared in our line of sight for a split second and I forgot them immediately. The unknown faces, so many stories etched in to each one of them.

We had passed through the region of Satar Mese with villages and towns whose names were yet to be printed on most maps. The Manggarai people living there had given us instant respect for undertaking this supposed pilgrimage to Wae Rebo. We had stopped at a roadside *warung* or small restaurant in a nameless village, whose claim to fame was to be the only restaurant for the next ten kilometres on either side. Three middle aged ladies were managing the place without any customers. They had relatively sharper features and claimed, "We are relatives of film actresses from India and Pakistan." They became very busy with preparing our food and there was a lot of activity all around in that small shack with wooden walls and benches with several eye shaped holes and gaps. One said, "The Manggarai people are very happy to meet foreigners but we can only speak Manggarai." Neighbours started coming in. Babies were held out to us to admire. People made way for a young man who sat on a bench facing us. His name was Arif and he could speak English. Arif looked Japanese with thick eye brows, "Iused to be a diving instructor in Maumere. I enjoyed working with the foreign tourists. I had to come back to this village to support my mother in the fields after my father's death." His father was from Jakarta but had ancestors back in India. Arif was not around when his father had died. "My mother is old and I don't want to leave her alone lest anything happens to her while I was not around." But he said, "I want to go to India someday and find my ancestral home. I want to do something for my relatives back in India but I don't know who they are and where they may be." He repeated a few times that he would one day go to India and find them out. He spoke slowly and looked sick and weak himself. There was some great sadness in his eyes. Other people in the restaurant seemed to be distant from him. He looked concerned, "Now I am stuck in this place, I may be slowly forgetting how to speak in English." His house was far from the *warung*, "I had raced on my bicycle to meet you when they had called me to inform that visitors had arrived who could speak English." He asked people for a piece of paper and pen to write down our addresses. No one responded. We scrambled within our bags to help him with what he wanted and he used that to also write down a letter for his friend in Wae Rebo, Matien. The letter said, "Please help my friends, we are all good here." Later at Wae Rebo, we did find a Matien but he had never known Arif. We kept the letter for another day. By then the food had come in, purple rice from the hills with a small piece of fried chicken and bowl of hot salted water. This simplicity was the best item in their menu and the ladies managing the place spoke at lengths about the good qualities of their local rice. Arif became silent and kept looking at the floor. Everyone started giggling again.

Unlike the other major roads of Indonesia and especially in Java, there had been no Pertamina stations or petrol pumps along the road in Satar Mese. This was largely true for Flores and Sumba where much of the gasoline is sold in two litre bottles neatly stacked in sets of three placed in multiple rows in a rickety wooden shelf. On top of them, a piece of cardboard ripped off from a carton box is hung, with the beautiful word "Bensin" or petrol scribbled on it. Against the rustic backdrop, the entire assembly looks like a golden abacus placed by the road just in case someone needs to take a stop and calculate something. But I was missing the Pertamina stations. Along the highways, they provided a break from long journeys, occasionally on treacherous roads. In the front, there would be a small clean store selling a few grocery items and small packets of salted and spicy fried snacks. At its counter, would be a small young lady, too shy to speak out the bill. And just around the corner, there would be clean toilets, one of the great pleasures of travelling in Indonesia. There is always a clean hole nearby to give something back to the mothership. And when it came to toilets, I also respect the Vietnamese for their most outstanding innovation, the toilet signs. Not many can appreciate this, but some people like me, with both arrogance and myopia, often get confused between toilets meant for men and women. To me, the symbols outside toilets: of man with the spread legs and a woman wearing a skirt, appear quite similar unless I look from real close-up which is embarrassing. Many times, I have indeed transgressed to commit the not so original sin. To avoid such confusion, the Vietnamese typically put a picture of David Beckham outside men's and princess-to-some-people Diana outside women's. Simple and amazing; biggest problems of life solved.

But on the way to Wae Rebo, the abacus Bensin set-ups didn't come up with toilets. For a man, a general lack of shame and evolution took care of it and the thick foliage around the roads provided great opportunities, bar the fear of snakes, the only disciplinarian for us men. And I, Emyl and Sil had revelled in the pleasure of doing all the right things at exactly the right time. But for Lobo, we had to knock doors to ask strangers if she could be allowed in to their homes. They always obliged, leading her to the secret garden with a humble smile while in the front yard, children gathered to figure out the eternal questions, who we were and why we were there. Whenever Lobo came out after such stops, she always had a victorious smile, followed by the woman who had led her just now; her head down with a content expression. Only the messiah knew what happened in between. Copious "Thank You's" and

"Byes" later, the children behind shouting joyfully, we were on our way again, to find the next toilet. Isn't that what all journeys are all about?

Gopal Bhar, the eighteenth century court jester in Bengal, India, had once explained to his king what the meaning of the journey of life was all about. When the king had asked him about his opinion on the most delightful experience in life, Gopal Bhar mentioned that it was the moment of shitting. Hearing this, the king became furious at Gopal Bhar and his detractors used the opportunity to humiliate down. A few days later, Gopal Bhar invited the king to his house to ask for his forgiveness. The king, who loved Gopal Bhar, also felt sorry for being too harsh on him and obliged. After a sumptuous spicy meal, a long conversation followed and the food worked its way down the king's bowels creating a great urge to shit. When the king, after long restraint, asked Gopal Bhar for the way to the toilet, Gopal Bhar said that his humble toilet was not worthy of the king's bum and he couldn't let the king suffer the humiliation of using it. A thousand entreaties and denials later, Gopal Bhar finally showed the king the way. After the act, the king came out with a glorious smile. Gopal Bhar asked the king if he had changed his mind regarding the most delightful experience in life. The king agreed full-heartedly and left Gopal Bhar's house after lavishing him with gifts as a reward for his wisdom.

The border guarding modern civilization from the enchantment of a trail to Wae Rebo was marked by a primary school. The road ended at the school and behind it, adjacent to the school toilets, a muddy trail wound upwards to meet the secluded village. The school toilets came in the form of three adjacent rooms, one marked "Female", one "Male" and one on the middle marked "Guru" or "Teacher". One of the teachers,

Blasius Monta, was around to give us a few parting words. He was a native of Wae Rebo who had played a key role in increasing the awareness about the village in Indonesia and securing donations to renovate the traditional houses in the village. He had rather fluffy cheeks, a sign of relative prosperity in Indonesia. Tall and avuncular, his mild confident demeanour reassured us about what lay ahead.

It was two in the afternoon and we needed to walk fast to make it to the village before nightfall. At the lower slopes, we met a dozen men and women coming down from the slopes. The men were carrying big loads tied at the ends of poles they were carrying on their shoulders. The women were carrying enormous gunny bags on tied by a cloth to their forehead. They were coming from Wae Rebo. These men and women were scrawny with bones deeply carved out of their faces. Their weather beaten skin was taut. They were small people and didn't seem to be able to stand straight, their legs always bent at the knees facing outwards. Their broad, red-stained teeth were ever grinning, revealing a few missing ones. They walked in nimble steps, lightly jumping over the rocks and mud.

Elaborate greeting rituals would happen every time we crossed paths with these villagers coming down. We would shake hands very gently, ask about their well-being, tell them of our origins and intent, engage in some small talk, and then shake hands again gently before moving on. One of the elderly villagers expained, "We are carrying coffee beans to sell in the town market. On our way up, we will carry rice, soap and other supplies from the market. We followed a simple rule; twenty five kilos when going down, fifteen kilos when going up."

After one hour of climbing, the boredom of tropical forests with their uniform colouration and blocked views was setting in. Sil, the younger of the two brothers, was always at the front. Suddenly, both Lobo and I realized that Emyl was the Stalker, straight out of the Andrei Tarkovsky classic where the Stalker takes two visitors to the Zone where legend has it that one's innermost wishes came true. Emyl, like Stalker himself, was always at the rear. Wae Rebo lacked that reputation but we still wondered what if Wae Rebo had such powers. What if Lobo didn't feature anywhere in my deepest wish?

Emyl was enjoying the place, taking pictures of the surroundings, blowing whistles to attract birds, singing to himself, generally lost from the context of being our hired help for the trip. *Keras* or apes were all around us but we knew this only from the sounds they were making. Emyl began mocking them by mimicking them and they replied. The trail was getting muddier as we climbed higher. We saw evidence of recent landslide at an adjacent hill. The clouds were gathering as well and we pondered what we could do if it were to rain. Emyl repeated the much repeated saying in Indonesia, "Don't think about rain and it won't come." Our bags had begun to feel heavier. Mountain springs gave us the occasional respite. The water was cold and sweet. And all of us discussed our dream making a living one day just by sitting by a spring and filling up bottles with water to sell to some distributor who would be just standing by to do the rest of the business.

Wae Rebo suddenly revealed itself! At one bend of the trail, amidst the mist, we spotted seven houses neatly placed in a circle in a small lawn crafted out towards the top end of a giant landscape that began with jagged peaks at one end that gently rolled over to sea at the other end.

Our necks turned a full half circle to view the entirety. From that distance, the hills appeared fully covered in grandmother's mittens and the grandmother in this case happened to love dark green. The hills were undulating as they fell towards the sea appearing like gentle folds in a long curtain. Candyfloss clouds slowly floated over them trying to spot their lost rain drops. All four of us got lost in our thoughts and forgot the presence of one another as we stood in a line and silently watched the village fuming from the mist and clouds. The call of the camera came soon and we got busy taking pictures of one another against the landscape. There was a spring in our feet and we hopped and ran towards the village.

The people of Wae Rebo saw us from a distance and the men arranged themselves in a circle at the centre of the village waiting for us. As soon as we crossed the gate of the village which was nothing more than a bamboo perched horizontally on two standing poles, we were led to this centre, slightly elevated from the surroundings. No greetings were exchanged though everyone gave us a big smile whenever we looked at them. Only the children started interacting with us. They took a particular liking for my beard which was a few days old by now. Lobo took the hand of a girl and rubbed it against my cheeks. She squirmed and withdrew as the other children rolled around in laughter. One man came and asked them to behave while Emyl whispered in my ears, "Please, this is a serious occasion." In this confused state, we heard one old man chanting in Manggarai. Emyl explained that they were greeting us with their typical ritual for welcoming visitors. Only now we realized that the entire affair of sitting in a circle as soon as we were visible was well rehearsed. A fire was lit at one end and a white cock was held in front of the chanting elder. We knew what was about to follow. Many dogs climbed up the podium where we were sitting; they too knew what would follow. In quick seconds, what was just now a live cock, struggling to break free, lost its neck to the cold blade of a thin and long machete. It throbbed for a while in the hands of the person holding it and his hands kept getting steadier as it lost its life. According to the universal custom, its belly was slit open and the positioning of its entrails checked to get signs about the future. I asked Lobo if she knew whose future was written in the positioning of our own entrails. She said it was probably the shareholders of McDonalds. As is the norm, the entrails turned out just fine. We would all be healthy forever. The cock was burnt in the flame and the warmth was pleasant in the chilly air. After this, everyone became relaxed and headed back to their respective homes. We were left alone for a while to walk around.

The village of Wae Rebo comprised seven huge conical houses designed in the traditional Manggarai style. There were a few modern houses as well with brick walls and tin roofs, but they were built outside the main circle and cleverly covered by the vegetation around to leave the unique beauty of the village intact. Legend goes that the man who found Wae Rebo had built only seven houses and so the village still allows only seven such structures. The villagers told us that there were over eight hundred people living in Wae Rebo but we could see a lot less. We were told that it is because many of the villagers did not always stay at Wae Rebo.

The villagers had shiny darkened skins from exposure. The men wore hoodies or fleece jackets with names of American universities written on them. Some of them wore a turban made by wrapping a thick cloth many times. The women were wearing loose fitting shirts. Both men and women were wearing heavy sarongs which some men dragged all the way over their heads to hide from the chill, which at Wae Rebo's elevation of eleven hundred metres, was getting chillier as the sun sunk more and more. These head-to-toe sarong covered men looked like giant bowling pins moving around in search of a strike.

That day being a weekday, only the very young children were around at Wae Rebo as on weekdays the older ones stayed at the nearest town with a school. The children were sitting in small groups, scattered around the village. In order to stay warm, they had withdrawn their hands from their shirt sleeves and covered their crouching legs with their t-shirts. With their potato-sack dressing, they were looking like smiling chess pawns waiting to be moved. The children's clothes were torn and looked dirty. Their biggest struggle was to hide the huge dollops of snot. The poverty of the village was quite evident. The children surrounded us to take the stickers we were distributing. Everyone took turn to feel my beard again.

We were asked to go inside the tallest house, the *rumah gendang* which was used for ceremonial purposes. Traditional Manggarai houses look like giant shaggy inverted cones. They could be up to ten metres tall with five stories. The entire structure stands on wooden stilts and the base underneath the floor is dug to make space for the the animals, chicken and pigs. The raised floor is made of wooden planks while the support for the roofing which also serves as the wall is made of slanted bamboo poles which form the cone. This is then covered with layers of a kind of local grass called *Alang-Alang* which gives the houses their smoked shaggy appearance. The door of the house is cut facing the raised altar at the centre of the village ground and four very small windows are cut at four ends through the *alang-alang* wall. Spaced wooden planks are used to form the different levels and while the first floor is used for sleeping and dining, the other levels are used mainly for storage of grains and other belongings. Inside the house, a thick bamboo with small slits cut into it is placed at the centre of this whole structure to serve as a precarious ladder to the higher storeys. The floor is circular as is the arrangement of the houses around the central altar because Manggarai people believe that the circle is a symbol of unity. One of the village elders joined us to explain, "The centre of the house is called *Ngandu*, the main entrance is called the *Paang* and the back is called *Nagung*. The *Paang* will always face the village altar or *kompang*." Wooden planks can be used to make small partitions in the living area to provide some privacy to married couples for their businesses. From the outside, the top of the house ends in a spear-like structure. For the *Rumah Gendang*, this structure has horned symbolic heads placed at the centre of the spear. On a misty day, the mist can be seen forming a soft envelope around these houses, slowly rising upwards, kissing the roofing and making it moist before evaporating into the skies from the tip of the spear. The kitchen is placed in a separate small house and so are the toilets and bathrooms for each house. Emil threw in his bit of knowledge, "All the materials for the house are procured from the surrounding jungles. Wae Rebo is the only remaining example of authentic Manggarai houses. All other villages in the region have become modern or half-imitations of traditional houses." He meant that these houses had brick walls and tin roofing and yet retained the shape of the traditional house.

It was very dark inside the *rumah gendang*. The elders of the village sat in a row down the centre of the circular floor facing the only entrance to the house. Over time, we realized that to keep staring at the door was one of the favourite pastimes at Wae Rebo. We sat along the wall next to the door facing the hosts. Because of the glare from the door, we were probably not even visible to the village elders. Behind the elders, a group of women seemed to be busy with some cooking. Two huge drums were hung inside the *rumah gendang*. These drums were used for ceremonial purposes. A young boy came in to serve us tea and coffee. Emyl and Sil were very tense, "This is a very important occasion because the *Kepala Kampung* is about to welcome us."

In the faint light, the *Kepala Kampung* or the village head, looked like an ethnic sculpture for he perfectly blended with the brown turban and the brown sweatshirt he was wearing. Two chickens were brought in. We knew their fate. Again, amidst the ceremonial chants, their entrails were checked and their arrangements confirmed the rosy future predicted by the entrails of the chicken slaughtered a while ago. Smelling the blood on the floor, a mother dog and her puppies stormed inside and all the elders sitting in a row raised their hands to shoo them away in one synchronized action that might have thrown a real challenge to those festival organizers in North Korea. The mother dog made another charge soon and this time the synchronization faltered and the chanting went into disarray. The mother dog and her puppies entered again. Tempers began to rise but this dog had read Bertolt Bretcht's *Mother Courage and her Children.*

The *Kepala Kampung* started addressing us in Manggarai. A young man broke off the rank of elders and sat next to us and started translating the *Kepala Kampung*'s words to Bahasa Indonesia, "I wish you well and also wish good future for the people in Wae Rebo, Ruteng and

Singapore." Emyl, our own *Kepala*, addressed him in return, "We wish well for the people of Wae Rebo and thank you for your hospitality." It almost appeared like a diplomatic meet with animated speaking followed by multidirectional translation. The formality was stifling. The *Kepala Kampung* threw some rice on the floor. Emyl said that the rituals were over. This time, mother Courage and her children were allowed in and they licked up the blood and the rice in front of us like white droopy-eared little devils. The dead chickens were passed on to the older women who had so far been indifferent to whatever was happening. Then, for the first time, Wae Rebo lost it stern codified impression. One by one, the village elders got up, knelt in front of each one of us to shake our hands and introduce themselves, then got up and knelt to greet the next one from our group. They all had Christian names. We were excited when one of them introduced himself as Matien and we showed him Arif's letter. He read it a few times, discussed with others, and then out of politeness, told us that it must have been addressed to some other Matien who lived a hundred kilometres further off. Emyl told us that we should offer the villagers some token gift as was the tradition and asked if we had a packet of cigarettes. Since we didn't have cigarettes we took the young translator to one side and gave him fifty thousand rupiah to buy from him two packets of cigarettes which we then gave to the *Kepala Kampung*.

In our present obsession with health, one of the great sources for male bonding is being slowly lost. Even a few years ago, travellers had obtained visit permits and all kinds of favours from stern officials and other strangers through the simple charm of a smoke. What does a nicotine-phobic traveller do to navigate his way around foreign hurdles? How does he make friends with other strangers in the most time-efficient manner? Signs are disturbing as what is increasingly being used as a tool for male brotherhood in the face of declining smoking habits is to show pornographic pictures and videos on mobile phones. From god-fearing Iran to remote provinces of east Java, I have felt the uneasiness of strangers trying to become friends with me over a clip of Jenna Jameson.

After the formalities were over, the young translator took us out to show us around the village. He was lean and tall with sharp features. With his turban and his sophisticated way of talking that was in some contrast to the blatant simplicity of the other villagers, bar the aged *Kepala Kampung*, he seemed to be the heir apparent for a position at the centre of the phalanx of sitting village elders. His name was Yos. Yos had ventured out of Flores and had worked as a labourer in the badlands of Malaysia, in a palm oil plantation in Borneo. Those years had been tough for him, all by himself, doing hard labour, far from the cool highlands he was used to. He had come back, equipped with some broken English and confident mannerisms that seemed to be a bit of a rarity in Wae Rebo. He was now the main interlocutor between the outside world and Wae Rebo.

Yos explained to us the ways of the world in Wae Rebo, the rituals of climbing up and down for hours, the difficulties of not having any doctor or other emergency help in the village and the compulsion to stay away from children to ensure their education. "Most of the villagers work in the coffee plantations along the hills around the village. We also chop woods from the forest, plant cocoa trees and make a drink from the palm trees down below to make some money." It was also an exception of a village given that there was no Christian shrine in the village despite Christianity being their nominal religion. "If someone falls sick, the person has to be carried on our backs all the way down." Their much cherished houses were also not that durable, lasting ten to twelve years if it had a good run. The fear of fire, that had played havoc with many traditional houses in Flores and Sumba and might have played a singular role in destroying the traditions of the local people, was always in their minds. "Electricity is only available for two hours at night. We bought our own generators. We don't have any television, radio or newspapers. Every family has a house in another village along the coast. Our children spend most of their weekdays there to go to the local school. So their mothers also stay there during weekdays." The only reason to live in Wae Rebo was purely to stay in touch with their culture and we found it hard to understand, just as Yos may have felt when he had left for Malaysia.

One by one, the stars popped up on the Wae Rebo sky. The clouds had slept by now and the clear skies presented another delight for us star-starved city dwellers from Singapore. Yos led us to the house which was reserved for guests. On the pathway between the bathrooms and the back entrance of the house, we came across a group of children whom we handed some stickers. The oldest in the group, a girl named Jessica, wanted more. With her sweet face, she tried all forms of cuteness to entice us to give her one more. But beforehand, we had established clear policies for distribution of stickers inspired by age-old principles of Marx and Kropotkin. Each one could have only one sticker under normal circumstances. Only if the child under consideration was the only one within our line of sight and if this particular child was especially cute and took a liking for the stickers, she could have two. If the children under consideration looked too glum or appeared too violent and uncontrollable and showed no visible signs of later life improvement, the entire group could even be denied the stickers, the only violence to Anarchist principles of never ending opportunities for redemption. If the parents of the kids looked too unfriendly, the kids could be denied stickers as well, the only violation with Marxist principles of one generation suffering from the sins of the previous generation. So Jessica had to be denied firmly with that cold smile.

We went inside the house and Yos sat at the centre, again facing the entrance, while we settled ourselves along the edge of the floor facing Yos. The *Kepala Kampung* joined us soon after and sat beside Yos. Both kept staring at the entrance while talking to us. Making eye contact was not part of Wae Rebo *adat*. They showed us their guest book. Till that date, there had been three hundred and fifty foreign tourists to Wae Rebo and over two hundred and fifty local tourists. I was the first Indian to have visited while there seemed to be some confusion whether Lobo was the first Chinese. We were also the first people to have visited from Singapore. We felt reasonably special in this world which was over thirteen billion years old.

The lone fluorescent bulb perched in the pole at the centre of the room was too weak for the space it was surrounded by. We were sitting on thin mattresses woven from bamboo skin by the village women. They also made stiff heavy blankets from the same material and pillows out of husk. The *Kepala Kampung* was smoking heavily. With our broken language, it was hard to talk about things more distant from the day-to-day and the mundane. Yos and the *Kepala Kampung* asked Emil and Sil about things in Ruteng. For every question of theirs, Emil was giving long answers, often repeating the same thing in different word formats.

Sil was playing the role of the younger brother, quiet and looking content to be where he was.

Lobo asked Yos how he had met his wife. "Ten years back, when I had come to Wae Rebo from Malaysia on a vacation, I went for a wedding at a nearby village, down below. There I saw her for the first time. That night, we went Disco, Disco. We met a few times after that. Sometimes we met in the jungle, sometimes, by the sea. Everyone got to know soon and one day the girl's parents invited me to their home." Once the difficult questions were asked, everything was settled. I considered his wife to be very fortunate to have a man willing to climb up and down a wet hill for four hours each way just to meet her.

All along the conversation, the *Kepala Kampung* and Yos kept looking at the entrance. Even though we were the first visitors from India, Singapore and probably even China, they were keener to answer our queries about their own lives than to know about us. On the other hand, this was the first time Emil and Sil were having the opportunity to properly engage with us, having spent most of the day before either driving or going through the strenuous hike. And we were charmed to realize that they had boundless curiosity about the outside world. They asked us an ocean of questions, "What languages do you speak in India and China?", "How do you say this?", "How do you say that?", "What is the price for this?", "What is the price for that?", "How did you two meet?", "How do you get married?", "What are your good movies?", "Who are your leaders and presidents?" As we answered their queries, their eyes twinkled and their heads nodded vigorously while the *Kepala Kampung* and Yos kept looking at the entrance. Perhaps, for the people of Wae Rebo, we were just two more additions to the list of three hundred and fifty foreign guests they had met. Probably the visitors came and asked them the same old questions about their houses and way of living. They knew what we wanted and they provided that with the chicken slaughter, the food and the often repeated answers. In the guestbook, I had seen names of countries like Poland, Romania, Chile, and Argentina. We were not exotic enough to raise their curiosity. Perhaps, isolation in this form had had a curious effect of over-exposure.

We made a foray to the kitchen where about ten women were busy with the cooking. Three fires were lit in that small room and it was hard to breathe inside. But the women were in their best of moods as they laughed vigorously and turned Lobo into a guinea pig for domestic training. But her role was just turning a ladle and churning things. One baby girl didn't take kindly to all the laughter and started wailing and the whole house got together to comfort her. The smoke was too thick and we felt that death was near. With smiles, we left promising to come back and cook the rest of the chicken.

Watching the cooking had raised our expectations. This was surely not Masakan Padang country and Lobo was willing to bet her life on her hope that finally we will be able to swim in a sea of vegetables because according to her all traditional people loved vegetables. There were many pots working for us in the kitchen. The presence of so many ladies managing the pots, the long time it was taking to prepare, and the general festive mood back there were making us believe that this would be one of the meals of our lifetime to talk about to friends and people we should show off to.

As we joined the *Kepala Kampung* and Yos again, the conversation went on at snail's pace and gradually we became silent, getting more and more anxious for the food. We disengaged ourselves and started counting seconds. I had already decided to ignore my vegetarian instincts and my discomfort at having witnessed the ritual slaughter of the chickens earlier. Finally, one by one, the younger girls from the group in the kitchen entered the room and began placing the dishes on the floor. There was thin soup of chicken with not many pieces of chicken inside, a vegetable dish looking very green and fresh, deep fried dried fish, deep fried yam flakes, white rice and a plate of finely chopped green chilli soaked in vinegar.

The people of Wae Rebo express their hospitality by bringing the food closer and closer to you. So every few minutes, Yos would get up and bring one of the dishes closer to us. After some time, his next such move would have placed the dishes on our laps and so I placed them further back for Yos to begin his game all over again. Lobo was delighted with the food even though it was very bland and simple, bar the chopped chillies. She ate a lot of vegetables and also took the fish even though she never liked eating fish. Soon she transferred all that serving of fish from her plate to mine, another person who never eats fish. As for me, I was happy with the chilli which I would rank as one of the best I had ever had. My passion for chilli had much to do with my upbringing in the state of Assam in India where some of the strongest chilli is cultivated. Retail chains from all around the world come to Assam to raise stronger and stronger chilli and local people compete in crazy competitions for who can consume the most amount of chilli and who has the might to rub the most number of chillies in to her eyes. Deep in my mind I was also content, for to me, this act of consuming only rice and chilli was to express my solidarity with the Indonesian literary maestro, Pramodeya Ananta Toer, who had spent his best years in a prison in Buru Island during the Suharto regime, eating only rice and chilli paste and an occasional lizard for protein.

We asked the women to join us for dinner but they declined politely. Later we found them having dinner in the smoke filled kitchen. That was the nature of things in Wae Rebo. Women would only be sitting behind the line of elders in the *Rumah Gendang*. They would be missing from the altar at the centre of the village called the *kompang*. And when the guests came, they would do the cooking out of sight, only appearing to serve or take away the dishes. However, it would be inaccurate to say that they were denied any respect. When we were leaving Wae Rebo, Emyl led us to the kitchen, knelt down and gave a long speech to the women to thank them for their hospitality and handed over the entire fees for our stay at Wae Rebo to one of the women.

The generator went silent a few minutes past nine and a girl came inside to place a kerosene lamp at *Ngandu*, the centre of the house. Some of the women with young babies came in and quietly lay down by one section along the rim of the house. We could carry on talking but Yos said that it would be best for us to leave by eight in the morning or even earlier to avoid catching the rain on the way down. Taking the hint, we arranged for our sleep. The men and Lobo were to sleep at one end of the house while the local women at the other end, everyone's feet facing the flickering lamp at the centre, forming a radial pattern. Lobo's nose came late to the party and announced its arrival with a few big sneezes. I followed the call of duty and covered her with four traditional blankets. Yos gave us a look of astonishment but I assured him that everything was fine. Emil and Sil had come with no bags or any extra clothing and in one swift movement resembling synchronized diving; they collapsed on their mats and began unsynchronized snoring.

It rained heavily overnight and the next morning the air was crisp and clear. People in Wae Rebo wake up early and by six in the morning, the villagers were already busy with drying the coffee beans spread out on giant plastic sheets spread around the *kompang*. Our hosts were seemingly desperate to make sure that we don't catch the diabolical rain by leaving early. Breakfast was served soon after we got up; the same items that we had had the night before. Yos and *the Kepala Kampung* were back at the centre of the room, looking at the entrance with their fixed gaze. They were not even blinking. Yos's child, a young boy, perhaps six or seven years old, came up to his lap and started moaning in a grumpy cat tone. Yos consoled him by moving his fingers through the boy's hair and covering him with his own sarong. The boy began purring. Yos' eyes were bright and powerful and with his turban and fixed gaze, he was looking like a king. The *Kepala Kampung* looked dark and frail sitting next to him. It was suddenly obvious to me why Yos had come back from Malaysia. In the dense plantations of a foreign land, he must have felt too small for the big world. In the thin long block of sunlight that was coming in the room from the small entrance, Yos appeared too big for this small world.

After breakfast, Yos quietly came up to us to show a printed rate card for our stay overnight. It was not a big amount but reasonably large given the context of Indonesia. There were of course no charges for Emil and Sil. The glorified hospitality of Wae Rebo, as was expressed through the formal speeches and welcome rituals were real for Emil and

Sil. For visitors like us, it was more of a transaction. Of course, we had been treated well and it makes all the sense in the world for them, already very poor, to recover the costs of providing us food. But somehow, the printed rate card didn't form a coherent statement with the profusion of speeches welcoming us to their homes. I felt rather sad for the slaughtered chickens.

We left the village looking back from time to time for one more chance to have the glorious view that had had mesmerized us when we were approaching the day before; the cute huts held in the giant folded arms of a lush mother nature. But I couldn't find that view anymore.

We walked back along the same trail and the soft and wet earth was gently slurping to accommodate our footsteps. There were no signs of any rain and not pressed for time, we started enjoying the small variations in the monotonous vegetation around. There at a corner was a small yellow flower looking at the trail for the short life it has. It reminded me of Guo Cheng's poem, "Nameless Flowers." Further down, a cocoa tree had spread its wings with several bright red fruits to celebrate a party. Young fern leaves were softly curling their hairy way up to adulthood. A slug was gently going downhill. The fast stream appeared again and gave us company for the rest of the journey. We asked Emil and Sil if there were any tigers around knowing fully well there weren't. Emyl, who had by now evolved into our eldest brother, elder by a few decades, assured us in his ever gentle and steady voice that there were no *harimau* or tiger in those forests. I loved the word *harimau*. Somehow it made the tiger very humble and approachable.

Things we had seen once before were passing by us again. Perhaps we will never see them again in our lives. And we won't probably meet

Emyl and Sil again. I looked at the brothers with that thought. I could only see the younger one's back who was again always in the front while Emyl was following us; he was looking around the forest with wide eyes.

Back at Denge, Blasius Monta fed us a simple meal of noodles and pink rice at his home in rather elegant setting, surrounded by a pastoral idyll. Next door, a chicken raised a small commotion by tripping over a washing line and bringing down the entire set-up with all the clothes. At a distance, I saw a giant buffalo eating grass rather disinterestedly. The children of Denge were overjoyed with the stickers we gave and posed for us with all the happiness in the world. In the meantime, an elder girl, probably ten years old, served us the food. She was quiet and there was an immense sadness in her eyes. We put on our helmets or *helems* and set off again for the long journey back to Ruteng where the caterpillar awaited us.

The rains began soon and at turns where the road went uphill, we met groups of men on bikes flying down from the other side like superheroes with their colourful rain sheets stretched out like wings and their heads covered in fuzzy *helems*. Rain coats are the only clothes which a man can wear in pink, orange and any other atrocious colour and still hold his head high.

Halfway to Ruteng, Sil's motorbike gave up. We managed to find a roadside repairman whose store was nothing more than a tin roof over broken wooden walls that looked more fragile than cardboard. The shop didn't have the tube that Sil needed and he took someone else's bike to find a tube from another shop a few kilometres away. There were a few more men with motorbikes at the shop, waiting for the rains to stop. A young mother with a baby boy joined in for some shelter. Three children joined in as well. The young shop owner, conditioned by Indonesian hospitality, offered us two plastic chairs to sit on and we rotated the chairs with the young mother.

That instant of the shop owner offering us the chairs, with his back gently bent in politeness and humility, was the essence of the entire trip. Strangers who owed nothing to us showing interest in our comfort while expecting nothing in return, wanting to know more about us, exchanging smiles, not showing any cynicism, irritation and indifference despite their poor lives; all these warmed our hearts and made us glad to be born as humans. This young shop owner, the baby girl who showed us the way in Labuan Bajo, the fishermen of Komodo resting at our boat to have a small chat with us, and many more such people along our trip; their warmth and simplicity put soft sealants over the several holes in my mind created by years of scepticism about the risks of human encounter. The countless stories and warnings served to us by my parents and other elders about the perils of talking to that stranger were falling apart in their assumptions. It became tempting to dismiss famous acts of violence in human history as myths. In this country where over fifty one per cent of people described themselves as "very happy" according to an Ipsos study, the memory and reputation of the same people having killed over half a million during the Suharto takeover and the slaughter and rape of people of Chinese origin after Suharto's fall, was struggling for space in my mind. I was falling for the charms of the graceful people I met along the way and the only way to retain my sense of sceptic sanity was to keep reminding myself of these pogroms.

From the rice fields across the road, we saw a young man struggling to move a rice thresher. He was being assisted by two teenage boys. As they came on the road, we saw that they were probably twins and were also wearing identical clothes. The two boys were very thin, had big malnutrition-hinting eyes and shabby clothes. They parked the thresher along the road and joined the crowd at the repair shop, standing quietly at the other end from where we were sitting. They were inspecting us with frozen eyes. We began distributing stickers again to the children waiting at the repair shop. Emil asked for one and lovingly put it on top of his helmet. He was now the centre of attraction as he explained the beauty and the importance of the sticker to the other bikers who had surrounded him to take a look at his glorified helmet. We had given him a sticker that was the flag of Bhutan. The other bikers looked at us with hope, too shy to say anything. We gave one to all of them. We were in two minds about giving stickers to the two boys with the thresher; they seemed too old to enjoy them and they didn't have a bike. But they stared glumly looking at the stickers held by the others. Lobo argued that if Emil and the other bikers could enjoy the stickers, so could they and we passed on two stickers to one of the bikers to pass it on to the two boys as it was hard for us to reach the boys in the by now crowded shop. But the biker kept them for himself. He twisted his mouth to make a clicking sound to tell us that the two boys didn't matter. We were furious because this was a violation of our distribution principle but it didn't seem like an issue to fight over with a grown up. From among the crowd, we could see the glum faces of the two boys. When the rain became gentler and we began dispersing, we called out to the two boys who were already on the road. Emil and Sil joined us to call them back. They looked back and saw us waving at them holding the stickers. In an unforgettable moment, big smiles appeared simultaneously on their scrawny faces, their big ears raised up the sky even further, and they jumped and ran towards us. Taking the bunch of stickers we offered them, they screamed with joy and ran back to the thresher. The young man with them who was waiting by the thresher smiled and gently nodded towards us.

Back at Losmen Agung, we were again among friends. Everyone congratulated us on the successful completion of our trip. We were given the welcome more suited to people who have come back from the Hajj or Umrah. But then, a trip to Wae Rebo was perhaps equivalent to the Umrah for the Manggarai people. The blanketed men who always watched television were still there just exactly as we had been seeing them. And we spotted our beloved Adi floating around the hotel with his frog steps, suddenly turning his head towards us to give us a quick nod and moving on to catch his next insect. We asked Emil and Sil to join us for some tea but they were reluctant to come in with their wet clothes. They left us saying they would come back soon to have dinner with us after they had changed and cleaned up. I realized that they may not have even rinsed their teeth over the last two days. We went back to our room and Adi hopped in soon dragging a barrel full of hot water. The shower I had afterwards would have easily counted among the top ten showers in my life.

Having a hot shower in any hotel in Flores is an adventure in itself. At Losmen Agung in Ruteng, upon request, the hotel boy Adi would deliver a plastic barell filled with steaming hot water. We had to mix it with the cold water in the tiled enclosure in our bathroom to make it shower worthy. But this tiled enclosure had to be first cleaned thoroughly to remove the mosquito larvae and other muck that had accumulated for decades. However, at the hotel in Bajawa, there was no such tank to store water. Instead, we just had a small plastic bucket that could hold only half a litre. We would first buy two half-litre buckets of hot water for ten thousand rupiah each. Once the steaming water came, we would undertake a Machiavellian task of using these two and the existing bucket in our bathroom to mix the water. We needed to apply the laws of thermodynamics and specific heat, resulting in an arrangement of three buckets filled with water at three different temperatures. We would first use up the half bucket that had the least warm water among the three. We would then finish its contents in a carefully timed fashion such that by the time it was empty, the water in the next half bucket, by following Newton's law of cooling, would be at exactly the temperature the water at the first bucket was at when we started. Accordingly, we had organized the third bucket as well. After enjoying the fruits of such ingenuity, we had such a satisfied feeling that we would spend the rest of the evening just quietly lying in our room.

And all the bathrooms in Flores have a heart shaped plastic pan, typically pink in color. These cultural icons of Flores have a long handle and can be used to shower and also for cleaning the bum after morning duties. There is also some controversy about its shape, some call it heart shaped while others claim it is inspired by the outline of a bum.

By the time Emil and Sil came back, I managed to call Gunung Mas, a bemo company, and make a booking for the van the next day from Ruteng to Bajawa, our next destination. This was an outstanding achievement in my mind and I explained to Lobo my feat in great detail a few times. For I had passed the ultimate 'new language' test; to converse with someone over the telephone. It is much more difficult than conversing with someone face to face because one can't use gestures anymore which are often similar across cultures. So over phone, I can't tell a person I am hungry by holding pointed figures to my mouth, or tell 'later' by making a grand wave from near the middle of my chest to the right for that matter. So my ability to book the tickets was a genuine triumph. Nonetheless, deep in my heart, I was scared that the bus may eventually not turn up because of some misunderstanding.

Emil and Sil looked very fresh when they came back; a kind of transformation through shower that I thought was only possible for rowdy kids. They took us to a restaurant selling mutton and chicken soup and indeed the food was better than what we had had so far in Ruteng. They began talking about their own families and how they had grown up. Their parents had given birth to eight children and Emil was the eldest, fourteen years older than Sil who was number seven. Three of the siblings were girls and two of them were already married. The other brothers had gone out of Ruteng to search for work while Emil and Sil took up ojek driving. Emil said, "Things are tough because we get only five thousand rupiah per ride and there are so many ojeks and bemos competing for business." Emil was married with four young children, two of whom had gone to Ende to study. He had met his wife in the church. Sil was still single and looking. He said, "I don't have enough money to propose to anyone." I could make out that he was interested in the young lady who was managing the restaurant. Perhaps that is why he had led his brother and us to this place. "I like women who are working and self-sufficient," said Sil. But she was a Muslim while he was Catholic. I was wondering if they could pass this barrier. Perhaps he could get some ideas from how Lobo and I had paired up.

The brothers hesitantly invited us to their home, unsure of whether we would be offended by their poor settings. I remembered my trip to the volcanoes of East Java a year back when while coming back from Kawah Ijen to Surabaya, my driver had invited me to his home at Surabaya. He had been excited all along the trip, treating each moment like a rollercoaster ride. And once I was at his home, he showed off his broken English to his wife by introducing his wife to me as "Your wife". Despite such risks, we agreed with enthusiasm to Emil and Sil's offer and we headed for their home after buying some gifts for the household. It was a fifteen-minute ride but well out of the small town that was Ruteng. Soon we were riding through complete darkness but we knew that we were no longer among strangers.

Theirs was a small independent house, with wooden panels for walls and a tin roof. There was a small cemented courtyard in the front where the brothers parked their ojeks. When Emil knocked on the door and shouted, "Come out everyone! Come out everyone!" a young girl quickly opened the door and ran inside. We went in and I had a feeling of déjà vu as it looked very similar to the hall of the house where I was born. The light was dim, there were calendars, old and new, everywhere, pictures of Jesus, a framed certificate of Emil's wedding, a glass table, a three-seater chair and a glass cabinet with a small television on top. The walls inside were flamingo pink. Emil and Sil were visibly excited and calling out to all. There were two more rooms and we could hear a lot of giggling. One by one, Emil and Sil got all the household members to come out, some covering their face in shyness, giggling all the while. Emil's wife came forward and introduced herself. She had an air of confidence befitting the head of the household. Emil and Sil sat down looking like proud soldiers who have achieved some great victory. Lots of pictures were taken and Sil was teasing his younger sister, "You are looking like a demoness in the pictures." She began beating Sil like every sister does to her brother. Emil, to show his command of things, asked the kids for a pen and paper. It took a long time to get one. Emil began drawing a Manggarai house to explain to us the structure, something he knew that we were familiar with already. After some time, he lost his way. We kept the paper nonetheless to keep his prestige. I was imagining how the whole family, eight people in total, slept in the small bedroom next to the hall. Clearly, my idea of privacy and solitude didn't apply here but Ruteng was changing my idea of happiness. A small kindly gesture, a little friendly interaction, a smiling nod from a stranger, all these were enough to feel good in life. When Lobo's nose began protesting after such a long day, we left their house. When we stepped out, we realised that the neighbours were waiting outside all along to catch a glimpse of us. Will we ever come back to Ruteng, a small town far from the crossroads of world shaping events, but the brightest of places nonetheless?

The land of stacked buffalo horns

Bajawa was our next destination, another hill town. Bajawa is some sort of tourism central for people living within Flores. The town's cold climate and relatively better accessibility has made it quite popular for corporate retreats and small conferences for privately and publicly owned organisations in Flores. Foreigners went there to visit the traditional villages like Bena, within an hour's drive from Bajawa, a lot more accessible than the likes of Wae Rebo. The travel books talked gloriously about Bajawa, some called it picturesque, some called it cute, words strictly denied to aspiring travel writers as per the expert's advice. It seems that the travel guides have obtained a monopoly over such words; lush, azure, crystal-clear, rolling hills, verdant, and the list goes on. It was almost tempting to switch allegiance to another language instead.

Earlier, in the morning at Ruteng, my heart was beating fast. Who knew what the lady over the phone had understood when I had booked the tickets? If things were not how I was imagining, I knew that the ever-forgiving Lobo would give me a gentle smile and rub my back. But what would I do to myself? But right when the clock hit seven, we saw Ronaldo peeping in to our hotel. Yes, it was Ronaldo again, the same man who had dropped us from Labuan Bajo to Ruteng. Delighted, I ran towards him as if I had met a long lost brother. He too, made a cool rap gesture like "Yo" to greet us. I was happier at the fact that I had passed the ultimate language test.

Both in Flores and Sumba, there are three ways to travel between towns. The most expensive way is to charter a car or motorbike, all for oneself.

The cheapest option would be to catch one of the several bemos that roamed between the towns. A slightly more expensive way would be to book a seat in a car or van that went by the name of 'travel'. These 'travels' were not very different from a bemo but they were less packed and they wouldn't circle around a town for hours to pick up passengers before heading for their destination. In that aspect, the bemos were infamous. Like birds of prey, they would hover around the whole town looking for someone with a bag and half a willingness to travel. One could get a bemo to anywhere within Flores or Sumba any time he wanted. Within ten minutes, it would be at his door. The passenger, who let's assume is a foreigner to this land, is delighted at this promptness and high service standard. At this point, the bemo would appear very spacious and a luxury. The bemo would start instantly, its driver joyous alongside the smiling caterpillar, and head off towards the direction of the destination. But then suddenly, it would make an unexpected turn into one narrow alley and stop at someone's house. Ok, so there is one more passenger; let me take a better row of seats before he comes in; so would think the first passenger. The driver has stepped out and begun conversing with the family which has come out of the house. It is yet unclear how many and who all are travelling. Many bags are brought out and the family keeps talking with the driver. Our passenger inside is perplexed. It has been half an hour already. Suddenly, the driver receives a call and everyone outside becomes busy. He gets inside and starts the bemo and one of the family members goes inside the house and fetches an elderly lady who had not been in the scene all along. She is the actual passenger. Farewells are said and sometimes tears are shed and she clumsily enters the bemo, instantly gives our first passenger a smile and then quietly sits down at one corner and compresses herself despite the whole bemo being almost empty. Yes, only Indonesians have the ability to compress themselves into a never-objecting huddle like no one else. Relief comes and the bemo moves on but it's now going back towards the direction of the first pick-up point. The driver sees someone with a bag and stops. She is going to some other town. The driver reasons with her why she should instead head for the bemo's destination. A friendly chatter ensues, smiles are exchanged and the engine is stopped. What has happened now? Not to worry, the lady outside knows another person who might consider going to the bemo's destination and so gives that man a call to ask if he is willing to start his journey now. The driver is thankful as the man has obliged and has asked the driver to come to his house after thirty minutes. The first passenger, let's assume he understands Bahasa Indonesia, had been hearing this and patiently recalculates his time of arrival. The bemo moves on to the end of the town where the man had been waiting. He is travelling with a pig and even though this has been done countless times over, a discussion ensues on where best to place the pig. He could be tied on top of the bemo but it would be quite an effort. What if the pig struggles while shifting, falls down and hurts itself? A better option may be to lug it inside in between two rows of seats and it too could be used as a seat. Soon after, the pig is happily lying on the floor of the bemo with two young boys sitting on its breathing belly.

After two hours of circling around the town, the first passenger is now squeezed into one corner. People are sitting on bags, cartons and of course, the pig. The first passenger is at his wit's end but is at least certain that they will be finally heading where they should have. But not yet, the bemo suddenly stops at the main bus terminal and the driver says goodbye to him without saying anything more and walks away. For thirty minutes, nothing happens. It's burning hot outside and the bemo is heating up too but no one is complaining because everyone has compressed himself or herself, Indonesian style. There is a state of numbness all around. A long-haired man appears from somewhere and takes the steering wheel and parks the bemo under the shade to give some comfort. The messiah disappears. Suddenly, another bemo arrives and unloads two passengers, a young couple. The long-haired guy comes back and takes the steering wheel. He is the real driver supposed to travel to the final destination. The one before was just hoarding passengers and learning the trade before he took on bigger responsibilities. The young couple boards as well. The man squeezes in astonishingly in the space between the driver's seat and the door, sitting on a wooden plank that can at best support half his posterior. The first passenger has no idea where the other half of the man's posterior has been stowed. The pig and the stuffed caterpillar are both smiling as the bemo finally hits the highway, and a cool draft of air comes inside.

There are no such hassles with 'travel' or the chartered yet shared vans. From our experience, they came on the dot, didn't go chasing for passengers if half empty, retained the same driver all the way through, and didn't entertain pigs while still accommodating stuffed caterpillars. But just like the cheap bemos, they retained one quirk, to paint images of voluptuous, half-naked, Bollywood-style women on their mudguards with provocative poses and glares. I was trying to imagine a young man cleaning those mudguards, tenderly wiping off the dirt from the breasts and waists to reveal the flesh. Perhaps, the whole purpose was to make this tough job a good enough career option.

The part of the trans-Flores highway between Ruteng to Bajawa is considered by locals to be the most beautiful stretch along the serpent's back. But for us, the road was rather treacherous. The rain had caused landslides recently and at certain stretches, vehicles struggled to maintain their direction as they skidded through like drunken bison. As we were approaching Bajawa, we were driving through clouds and Ronaldo was bound to turn off the music so that he could focus. Now that was a serious thing because Ronaldo loved his music, the high-pitched screeching sound coming out from the bemo stereo. The headache-inducing cacophony was barely distinguishable from the sound of some crazy machine hammering a tree and scratching a glass at the same time. But Ronaldo's clean-shaven head kept bobbing up and down to this and sometimes he would suddenly lift up his hand and guide it like a flowing river to follow the song's journey for a while. Since the same songs were coming back again and again along the four-hour journey, over time I understood the language of the glass scratching. Some of the songs were in Arabic, some in English, some in Bahasa Indonesia and some in Hindi too. Ronaldo was very international and eclectic in his tastes. My head felt like a boom box as we got down at Bajawa, another of those typical four-hour journeys which actually took us six.

Bajawa was another town full of strangers and we didn't know where the unknown streets went to. I felt like a beat poet, only a few generations obsolete. I had first read the beat classic, Jack Kerouac's *On the Road* when I was sixteen and found it of little appeal. Truman Capote had said about the book, "That's not writing, that's typing" and it was indeed arduous reading for a non-American. The blurb of the book had a quote from Kerouac's fellow beatnik, William Burroughs, "The alienation, the restlessness, the dissatisfaction were already there waiting when Kerouac pointed out the road". And when I read *On the Road* for the second time, ten years later, when I was working and financially well placed, I fell for it completely. After a few pages, Kerouac got me 'alienated', 'restless', and 'dissatisfied'; and I am not sure if those feelings have vanished yet. I made countless plans to hit the roads in India on a shoestring budget, looking out for bullock carts and trucks for transportation, seeking out unknown villages, and sleeping under trees; but never dared to take the leap. The closest I came to the idea of *On the Road* was during separate backpacking trips at Copenhagen, Stockholm and New York. And still, the memories of bunk beds, rats in six feet by ten feet hostel bedrooms, common toilets with no doors, sleeping in railway stations, buses that come back half way through their journey, are the most cherished that I have. The whole pointlessness of the journeys in *On the Road* seemed to be the point of it all. The book made me believe that the best way to spend the arduous time between a pointless birth and a much delayed death is to travel, to seek out the new and the unexpected. In my fantasy world, I was Neal Cassidy, living just for the moment, an aspiration for myself and the rest of what I considered an ignorant world. But then, the Beat and the following hippie movement brought about an uproar and then died without leaving much of a trace. *On the Road* has been replaced by *Seven Habits of Highly Effective People*, the 'stream of consciousness' typing has been replaced by repeated bludgeoning by business phrases such as 'pro-active' and 'core competency'. After all, the 'road' itself has been replaced by expressways where asking for a joyride almost certainly means death.

The name Bajawa sounds rather harsh and when we reached, the town was surrounded by dark, gloomy and bushy hills. But the little town of fifty thousand people does have a tourist hot spot, a very short stretch where the road peaked to fall down gently on both sides. At this road peak, on one side was the Edelweiss hotel, the prince charming of Bajawa. On the other side was Hotel Korina, with a darker lobby, crusty wooden doors, an older shade of paint and with rooms half the price. Around these hotels were a few restaurants selling western fare, schnitzels and pretzels and all zels, but still having the look and feel of a *masakan padang* dig. And in between these glorious establishments, the pride of Bajawa, facilities that clearly established it as the snooty queen of Flores tourism; the touts ruled, hunting for anyone looking out of context to sell them a package. A package! That was an alien concept for us who have thus far been used to the rough and tumble of travelling in Flores where every aspect of traveling is some form of negotiation with little to arrange off the shelf.

When we arrived, these touts were playing some form of soccer on the road's peak. A bunch of young man who looked straight out of Jamaica with their dark features and knotted long hair, stopped their game and attended to us as if they had been waiting for us all along. "Come to Edelweiss", "Sign up for the package tour to traditional village." Interestingly, with all these packages, only two seats were left, at atrocious prices. "You have to book fast else you would be left stuck in your hotel rooms and tomorrow you can't watch our soccer game also because all of us will all be gone with our clients." We acted fast and ignored them all with our meaningless smiles, well-practiced from dodging credit card sellers in Singapore. After Emil and Sil, we could settle for nothing less. We would need to find the brothers of Bajawa.

By now, we had become expert hotel hunters and decided to check out all the options before choosing one. We settled for Hotel Korina because it seemed so shy to get some new business. The place was managed by a petite young lady. We searched all the rooms for someone to take our booking and found her in the bathroom of one room, all too tangled with her cleaning gear. Always head down, with just a hint of a smile, she showed us a few rooms, and Lobo diligently checked the mattresses in each for their right firmness. At first she would sit on them, then bounce about a bit, then lie down, then change sides, then get up and give a few deep squeezes to the hapless mattresses. The ones we rejected kept facing the roof in want of respect. She did find one to her liking and collapsed there immediately, in love with the world.

When we came down for lunch, the soccer players had disappeared. There was not much to do for that day and we headed to the main market or Pasar Bajawa. The roads went up and down with funny statues at the crossroads. At one crossroad, there was the familiar couple greeting visitors with folded hands and wary looks. At another, there were the again familiar statues of schoolchildren, one boy and one girl, asking the nation to move forward with small flames in their hands that again looked like vanilla ice-cream on cones.

Small hills surrounded the town, giving it a Rio de Janeiro feel sans the bustle. All the same, Bajawa has an edgier feel to it than Ruteng or Labuan Bajo. There was graffiti on the walls. Many young men were loitering in the streets. There was even a shop selling big masculine stickers for motorbikes. We wondered if we could stock up on the stickers we gave to children but the only options were skulls and bones.

We had been put off a bit by the town, which lacked the charms that the travel books had claimed, no colourful gardens and people still looking at us tourists with dollar signs on their minds. But our hearts warmed up as soon as we entered the Pasar. I was looking for an extension cord and entered a hardware shop. A plump Muslim lady wearing a headscarf was manning the shop. She was sleeping contentedly, mouth gaping open. But I could see that she had exactly the thing I needed. We stamped hard on the floor but her mouth opened wider. We rustled some stuff in her shop but withdrew soon lest she thought we were stealing. We coughed, and coughed, and coughed. She woke up with a start and somehow immediately converted the gaping mouth to a huge smile, making the town instantly friendlier.

The market was like any other Flores market, with shops organised according to what they were selling. In every such market, the stalls selling meat and dried fish are the ones that attracted my attention the most. The sight of the flattened bodies of the dried fish stacked up neatly, their colours fading and resembling earth more and more, their eyes still alive and questioning like dead fish's eyes always do, and the pervasive stench that hints at the presence of their spirits, intrigues me and makes me wander around them even though I have nothing to do with them. Somehow in Flores, these stalls for dried fish occupy centre stage unlike the meat shops which elsewhere in the word are hidden behind some corner. In small towns like Bajawa, the violence of slaughtering animals is more up close to the buyers. Chickens packed in bamboo baskets look at us with crazy eyes hoping that we wouldn't be choosing them. Just above their basket, on a moist wooden table, some of their brothers had already been skinned; looking like tender human babies but headless and with lifeless claws, small splotches of blood around them, fast drying up.

In Flores towns, one rarely sees meat of big animals like goat or cows on sale because people are too poor and these animals too precious for daily consumption. So they are reared for ceremonies and festivities with buying and selling happening through contacts rather than through the *pasar*. We move on from the terrified chickens but their respite is short lived as another group of potential eaters of their flesh walk by.

The section for vegetables and fruits was relatively big, compared to what we had seen in Ruteng and Labuan Bajo. They came in dazzling greens, reds and oranges, and Bajawans have a penchant for arranging fruits and vegetables in neat conical groups. All of them are run by women and they were delighted to see us. Calls poured in from all over the aisle inviting us. Having suddenly become stars of *pasar*, we became snooty and took our time to move from one shop to another, denying the waiting women their thrill of canvassing their wares to us. Lobo was excited as we bought all varieties of fruits. We would be consuming fruits for a long time. Lobo came up with the idea that since the restaurant owners of Flores never came to buy vegetables, we should instead take the vegetables to them. We found a very old lady squatting at one corner with only a bunch of papaya flowers to sell. We had never eaten papaya flowers but the lady looked miserable and the flowers looked fresh and beautiful as a bunch. She was past her days of sanity and her neighbour came over to complete the transaction. She advised us to boil the flowers with rice and guaranteed us a delightful meal. We came across a line of women, all squatting, each one picking lice from the one sitting in front of her. They had probably closed their shops already and it was their time now to bond socially. And then we met Mama Mena.

She must have been watching us for a while and we heard her calling us loudly. She was a middle-aged woman sitting by the boundary wall of the pasar, selling fruits along with other vendors in the row. She had dark skin with chiselled features, unruly hair and red-stained teeth that were perpetually grinning. She just wanted to draw our attention and know where we came from. "I just have a small collection of chillies, onions and ginger," she said. She had neatly arranged these in cones in her ramshackle shop, which was little more than a large plastic sheet over four sticks. The lady next to her stall was her sister who was selling all kinds of fruits. "We are both married in the same family but I lost my husband a few years back." "You are extremely pretty," both the sisters exclaimed to Lobo. Then they looked at me and began rubbing their noses, "Your nose is very sharp." That was enough to bring out big smiles from us and we sat along with them. "We come from a villages near here. When the day is ove, we will wrap all these fruits and vagetables in this cloth, and take an ojek home. The next day, we will come back early in the morning with all these vegetables and fruits. There is only one bemo which comes from our village to this town," explained Mama Mena. "Business is slow today," she said, but they both looked happy. We asked to buy a handful of passion fruit which they called *markissa* but they filled a whole bag with *markissa*, guava, and bananas for the same price. "These will get spoilt anyway," Mama Mena reasoned with us. The warmth of Flores that had charmed us so much in Ruteng was acting its way through our hearts in Bajawa as well. But we had to move on for our dinner and to find the brothers who could take us around the next day. The sisters of Pasar Bajawa called back, "Promise that we will visit us again tomorrow."

We were looking for ojeks to take us around the next day. There were many around Pasar Bajawa, all giving us that familiar wink in hope for business. We approached one, all of four feet tall, wearing a very fluffy oversized jacket and an oversized *helem*. The motorbike was too big for him and with his small moustache, he looked like a tame version of Hitler. Well, perhaps the conspiracy theory about Hitler having escaped to Flores was after all true, and this man was one of his progeny. But Roni looked extremely harmless and so we felt most comfortable approaching him first. After he understood our requirements, he gave an astronomical price, "One million rupiah." We walked away and he came running after us like a penguin to take our offer of twenty thousand rupiah for two ojeks for the whole day. He also had a brother who drove ojek, perfect for us, because we loved travelling with brothers.

As we were looking for a place to eat that first night in Bajawa, our usual challenges came up. The choices were just as limited as in Ruteng and we didn't want to indulge in the tacky European offerings near our hotel. Two old women called out to us and showed us a restaurant nearby, vouching for its quality. The two ladies were looking very photogenic, dressed in traditional ikat of the local Ngada tribe, and I couldn't control my temptation to take their photographs. But for some reason, one of them was vehemently opposed the idea, "No, no, no, no, no!" A young man came out of the restaurant and tried to convince her, "You still look very young and pretty and that's why foreigners want to take your picture. They want to show it to film producers in their home countries. You could soon be in English movies." But she refused hysterically, "No, no, no, no, no!"

Inside, the restaurant was rather queer, and not just because dog meat soup was the first item on the menu. It was divided into two horizontal halves. The front half had benches and tables for people to sit while the remaining half was raised one foot higher and served as the bed for the family. A wooden cupboard stood in between the two halves, where biscuits were on display for sale. On the time-worn menu, the first item was dog meat soup, with its ink fading.

We asked the ladies managing the place if they could do something with the papaya flowers we had bought. They exclaimed, "Why have you bought such an expensive vegetable? And you have bought so much!This is best used in very small quantities mixed with other vegetables because the taste is very bitter." As expected, just like any Indonesian restaurant, they didn't have any other vegetables. So they said they would try to boil it a few times in salt water and drain the water away so that the bitterness is gone and perhaps we could dip the boiled flowers in chili sauce to get something out of it. We agreed and ordered some chicken soup. All over Flores and Sumba, there is very little meat in these soups and the potions were always small. That partly explained the lean physiques of the local people, the other reason being their daily hard labour. The vegetables were as bitter as the devil would like to have and we left it looking splendid and fresh as a conical heap of flowers.

As the night grew, Bajawa turned holy. Restaurants were scrambling to close and make space for evening masses, from each of which the bee-like buzz of holy choir singing started coming out. We were still charmed by the Bajawa market and went around looking for things we didn't need. We stocked up on our stickers. We had to choose between teenage saviours of the world, Ben10, Hello Kitty, Mermaid, Doraemon and Barbie. After much uninformed debating about the virtues of all, we settled for Ben10 for the boys and Mermaid for the girls. A young girl sold us a variety of biscuits from her ramshackle shop. Next door, at a surprisingly sleek juice store that had no customers, we came across a giant papaya. Most of the shops were closing down; it was already eight at night. Only the shops catering to the youth, those selling music CDs and motorcycle gear were still shouting out psychedelic lights with blaring music. One clothes shop was still open and Lobo decided to check out Indonesian ethnic wear, the *kebaya*, for herself. The owner and her assistant, both Muslim, wearing headscarves, began taking non-stop about how glorious Lobo was looking with each dress. They resorted to clapping soon and I left Lobo with them to check out the mannequins.

I have always been intrigued by mannequins. When I see them, I can't resist the temptation to play with their heads, from looking under their skirts, and holding their hands. Mannequins are flourishing as a species, courtesy the bloom of shopping malls worldwide, their protected reserves. Mannequins also live a life more hallowed than the wealthy and the privileged, getting to wear the gilded clothing and jewellery for much longer than their actual owners. But the thing that's troubling mannequins is a mysterious disease that has led to them being born with deformed bodies. So many of them can now be seen without heads while some have only thighs and posterior. This disease is called cost cutting.

Late that night, Emyl messaged us to convey his good wishes and asked if we were comfortable. The next day, Roni and his brother were missing at the scheduled time. When I called Roni, I could only hear a garbled response, coming from someone in deep sleep. I tried again, by when Roni must have already been dreaming of something else for the garbled response now sounded different. After waiting for half an hour, we decided to head for the market to pick up a new pair of ojek brothers. Halfway to the market, we saw two ojeks flying down from uphill. Roni looked genuinely relieved, his brother more sceptical of us strangers.

Following standard operating procedures, I rode behind the younger brother while Lobo sat behind Roni, the safer looking animal. His brother, Joseph, was a lot younger, stronger, darker, gloomier, perhaps annoyed at being woken up for work. We were heading to Wao Muda, where recent volcanic explosions had led to formation of a crater with three coloured lakes, occasionally blue, red, yellow or green. The town soon gave way to forests with secondary vegetation, tall trees with small villages in between. When we reached the village of Wao Muda, a dozen people surrounded us. One of them, a young man, spoke out, "I speak English, guide." Now that one can read everything about a new place online, we already knew that the trail was well marked, not requiring a guide. Nonetheless, we thought of having some company, lest we get lost and lose some more time, given that we were already late. The man's name was Marcel and he asked for an atrocious hundred thousand rupiah. Within seconds, he agreed to thirty thousand and would probably have given away more if we had persisted. The other villagers just looked at us, smiling quietly while we negotiated with Marcel. Marcel looked like a character straight out of Cape Verde with dark skin, short curly hair, and thick beard set on an angular face. We followed him on the narrow muddy trail, the colour of dark chocolate mixed with wet coal, surrounded by thick wet grass.

It was soon obvious that Marcel didn't know any English other than saying, "I speak English, guide." And he wasn't very keen to talk in Bahasa Indonesia either. He perhaps believed in being a silent guide, one from which we were supposed to know about a place through our own conjectures. He kept walking fast, maintaining a big distance from us and we would need to scream to ask him anything. About ten minutes later, we heard footsteps behind us. We were being followed by two young men who seemed to have appeared from nowhere. It was already thick forest and our hormones for suspicion were triggered. I introduced myself to the young men and they seemed quite clueless as well as to why they were following us and who they were. They didn't even speak Bahasa Indonesia. Marcel explained that they were not from the region and that didn't help calm down our suspicion. Soon two dogs appeared and they began following us as well. Lobo, a self-proclaimed befriender of all canines, became delighted with this and pretended to be able to communicate with them. But my anxiety with the whole situation continued. Was Marcel involved? Where were they leading us to? Should we walk behind the whole group so they can't attack us from behind? But the two young men looked too lost and lacking in confidence to be of any serious threat. When we paused, they paused. When we tried to engage the dogs, they waited. This continued for half an hour. I was reminded of the Hindu epic Mahabharatha wherein the five victorious brothers and their shared wife climb their way to heaven and one by one, they succumbed and died because they all had committed some sin in life; except for the eldest, Yudhisthira, and his dog. The dog was actually Yudhisthira's father. Dharma, or Principles. Who was the Yudhisthira among us and which of the two dogs was Dharma?

We climbed on and on and the mist enveloped us. Everything looked soft, tender and heavenly, whether it was a broken twig or cow dung. Thick bushes of long grass enclosed us for some distance. In the haze, we saw a cow looking at us with its big eyelashes. A few metres further up, a lonely house was standing on stilts in between pillars of tall trees, exciting in us a sudden urge to consider it as our residence after retirement. Next to it, a horse, glowing with health, was gently sniffing at the grass. The narrow trail was now in a more open territory and the two young men with the dogs branched off to go downhill. We asked Marcel about them. Marcel guessed that they may be hired hands from more remote parts of Flores who helped the farmers from this village. That explained their clueless looks and I sighed, wishing I had been warmer to them.

As we came closer to the crater rim, we went past several shrubs with those delightful mountain flowers that bloomed just for their own sake. When we reached the viewing point, all we could see was a huge depression filled with soupy mist. Suddenly, Marcel began talking a lot, in Bahasa Indonesia, "It is really unfortunate that we can't see the lakes. I had not hoped it to be like this as even on such cloudy days, they can be seen. I had come here just a day before and the lakes were visible. Would you like to go back now?" We didn't care much, sat down on the grass and took out pandan flavoured cakes and offered him a piece. He gave out a big laugh and thanked us for our offer saying, "Fasting, Fasting." He had probably been anxious all the while that we would be mad with him for having brought us up for a price while knowing that nothing would be visible.

Marcel was a farmer and explained the lakes just as much as a farmer would know about volcanic lakes, "They have colour because of volcano." The lakes got the colour from the salts from the earth. During the dry season, they would evaporate completely. They were small features, perhaps smaller than half the size of an Olympic swimming pool. Sometimes there were three lakes, sometimes five. They were only ten years old. As such, there were no myths surrounding them yet. At the rim, which fell off sharply to the cloud-filled abyss, we enjoyed our end of the world moment with a farmer pretending to be a guide.

The farmer in Marcel revealed itself fully soon as he became our link to the forest. He ran around the rim looking for leaves of a plant called *Kayu Putih* which he said did wonders to the skin of young and old. He tore the leaves into small pieces and asked us to rub it over our faces. Lobo, with her Chinese roots, ever eager to believe in the healing powers of every plant and animal, immediately followed his advice and insisted I follow as well. Marcel continued his role as the brand ambassador for *Kayu Putih*. He said, "People from all around the world, especially the Chinese, came to my village to take *Kayu Putih*. It can cure insect bites, itchiness. It will make you fairer." Earlier Marcel had observed me profusely scratching my beard, two weeks free from the blade. He said, "Kayu Putih is good for *gatal-gatal,* instantly." By now, Lobo was forcibly rubbing the leaves on my face. I didn't mind the raw smell of nature on me and encouraged, Marcel began pulling more and more leaves. My bag was full of them and when he gave me one whole branch, there was no option for me but to fasten it to my backpack like a flag mast. Then Marcel asked, "Do you want to take a few plants back to Singapore," and headed to the infant trees to pull them out. At this point, Lobo finally asked him to stop and he relented.

Marcel also introduced us to *Kayu Manis*, whose fragrant sweet bark could be used for cooking, He scratched and pulled out some and made us taste. He explained to us the various berries and the flowers that came along the way as we climbed down with the mist. Just like all village people who love to talk about how they brew alcohol, he too proudly talked about the palm wine they made from the female palm tree. Along one section of the trail, came tender vines of Japanese *Labo Labo*, a form of vegetable very popular among the locals. Suddenly, Marcel disappeared among the trees. We heard rustling and saw him appear precariously balanced over a thin branch sinuous from his weight. He grabbed a few branches and jumped to the ground, tearing them off in the process. Like a precocious kid, he held out in front of us a dozen or more passion fruits. In the mountain cool, the fruits were delightful and Marcel also ate one *Markissa* even though he claimed to be fasting. It seemed like everything from the forest could be eaten or used and I got particularly attracted to one kind of orange-colored berry and reached out to consume it. But Marcel rushed to block me from the plant for some mysterious reason, "No, no, no, please, no," making gestures that people make when they are trying to separate two people fighting in the streets. This surely couldn't be hemlock?

We passed by the cow with the kohl-lined eyes and Marcel and the cow chased each other in circles for a while. We met Marcel's wife passing by and also his uncle and another village native. Marcel asked all the usual details about us, "You know that the pastor at the village church is also from India. He has been living in Bajawa for many years. Let us go and meet him." When we reached the church, it was closed and the pastor was out. One the way to the church, Lobo had tripped and twisted her ankle. She complained that this was the easiest hill we had trekked together and this is where she had to trip.

Back at the point from where we had started our hike to Wao Muda, I founded the dirtiest toilet in the world behind the village church. It was a flies' paradise and even I, usually indifferent to hygiene concerns, had to hold on and keep the faith that another toilet would emerge soon. This toilet at Wao Muda was the site of the devil's revenge as he fled the earth taking the exit behind the church.

When we came back to Bajawa, we invited the ojek brothers to have lunch with us but they were very hesitant. They would just look around, then at each other, and then at us, whenever I asked them what they wanted to have. They waited for us to order and just repeated what we asked for. We tried to strike up a conversation. Rony, being the elder brother, answered in short syllables, while his younger brother kept looking at us, scared. They relaxed only after we took the initiative to pay for both of them. We headed on to the Ngade heartland of Bena.

Bena is a small village, with around forty houses placed in rows forming the edge of a mango-leaf shaped slope, rising up to end at an altar that looked over a spectacular cliff surrounded by folding hills falling into the sea like stacked ham slices. Unlike the circular obsession of the Manggarai, the Ngada architectural system relies on edges. A cuboidal wooden facade rests on a square platform and supports a huge triangular roof made of grass. Skulls of buffaloes with their giant horns are stacked up in the front of most houses as a symbol of prosperity.

Jaws of pigs are also hung on railings. They skulls and the jaws have a certain masculine beauty about them even though their origins were macabre. The village of Bena is not as splendid as Wae Rebo but its relative accessibility has made it more popular. Nonetheless, we were the only tourists at that time in the village. Later, we learnt that there was a registration counter where a small donation is the norm for tourists. Unaware of this, we walked straight in. Most of the adults were away from the village, working in the fields. The children, as usual, opened up to us, once we offered them the stickers. They were distinctly poorer than any we had encountered so far. Many were walking around naked. A young man was playing with a puppy while some dogs were sitting gracefully on the holy stone blocks. At the altar, at the highest point of this village, there was a viewing point where the walls and chairs were scribbled with abuses and vows, giving the place the prestige of a heritage site. When we were heading back, old women called out to us, asking us to buy dried vanilla sticks from them. Some hesitantly held out ikat cloth hoping we wouldn't be interested. A baby girl got very excited seeing us and tried to kiss Lobo, making her all wet with her saliva. We left as silently as we had come.

Our next destination was the village of Nage, another traditional village about seven kilometres from Bena. But these seven kilometres were kilometres from a video game. Meteoric craters were strewn every five metres, filled with stale muddy water that came into monstrous life when the motorcycle went over them. Where the craters were absent, slippery pebbles tried to push us down. Roni and his brother struggled to navigate the ups and downs while we were bobbing up and down as if on pogo sticks. What I thought would be a ten-minute journey took us an hour as at many places, walking was safer than riding the bike. When we reached Nage, I found Lobo shell-shocked. She said that for the first time in life, she had felt as if she was going to die. On the way, we had passed a river that carried steaming hot water from a hot spring. Unlike many of the East Asian nations, there were no glamorous *onsens* or spas located around this. A group of noisy naked children were having a hell of a time in the hot flow.

Nage rarely received any visitors and as soon as we entered its premises, children surrounded us. The houses here were arranged haphazardly unlike Bena. Some of the houses had also sacrificed the grass roofs for cheaper tin structures. From the village, we could see the Fuji-like near perfect cone of Mount Inerie, breathing quietly over us from so near that if she was to give out a sudden belch, life would be short. The men of the village had come back from the fields and were playing cards. This was the first time Roni and his brother had come to this village so they also joined us to explore Nage. At Bena, they had stood by their motorbikes which they had parked outside the village compound.

People of Nage seemed a lot poorer than in Bena as evident from the children's clothes. But they were also more charmed by us. As we crossed the houses one by one, the families lounging outside engaged us in some small talk. The family in the last house, at the edge of Nage, invited us to have some tea with them. The man of the house sat in front of us in a crouching position, a posture near universal among villagers. He had an intellectual's eyes and voice. The women of the house brought out their babies for us to admire. Children invited us to join them in the national game of Flores, to keep rolling a used bicycle tyre with a stick. The whole of Nage looked on with high expectations as

Lobo took control but she performed disastrously. I decided to avoid her fate. One girl, probably seven or eight years old, was particularly fascinated by us. Quietly, she followed us all the time we stayed at Nage. One of her eyes was still. She would probably grow up to be the most beautiful woman in Flores.

We learnt a lot about the culture of the Ngada people by talking to these villagers. Ngadas are often classified as house societies as defined by the legendary anthropologist Levi Strauss wherein an ancestral house serves as a focal point of defining economic and familial relationships. The intellectual-looking man had explained, "Every Ngada refers to their house as their origin." A Ngada house has two symbolic structures in front of their house. A husky umbrella-like structure called *Ngadhu* is the symbol of the male force. Faces are carved on the central pole supporting this structure and many rituals need to be followed during its erection. The man told us about this pole "A priest selects the tree from which it is carved. The carving is done outside the village. When it is brought inside the village for installation, the women are required to stay indoors to avoid bad consequences." The female force is represented by the *bhaga*, a small replica of their typical residential houses. People often crouch inside the bhaga and pray to the ancestral spirits. The village complex is also typically strewn with irregular stone blocks and stone pillars which were once used to mark graves before Catholic influences stopped the practice of burying deceased family members in front of the house. One villager bemoaned, "Many of these stones are hundreds of years old. But some have been stolen away to construction sites around Bajawa." This was relieving the dead of their weight but fading them from living memory at the same time.

The rapid spread of Catholicism in Flores is one of the most glorious episodes in the history of missionary efforts. In less than a hundred years, the entire island was flooded with crosses and statues with sorrowful expressions as over ninety per cent of the disparate population of Flores turned Catholic. According to the anthropologist Susanne Schroeter, in the case of the Ngada, the missionaries adopted the approach of emphasizing the similarities between the Ngada and the Catholic worldview to foster this conversion. For instance, they kept telling the Ngada people that they were monotheistic by showing similarities between their traditional supreme God, Dewa, to the Christian god. This, despite there being many smaller spirits in the Ngada pantheon including Nitu who stands for mother earth and who used to play a key role in Ngada myths.

In a short time, a syncretic system developed under which the people adhered to Catholic ways for day to day living while still following certain traditional rituals, especially when it came to unexpected death from unnatural events. In such instances, elaborate funeral rituals involving extensive animal sacrifices were practised and the ancestors were enlisted to fight back the evil spirits or *polos* responsible for such deaths. The obsession with ancestors and polos affects much of Ngada life. These dual forces provide a certain feeling of timelessness to what is an uncertain and short life by providing a layer where those dead can interact with those alive and those dead can still influence turn of events, albeit with more powers. One of the villagers said, "The powers of ancestors can help in fighting off the *polo*. But if the ancestors are angry, they join with the *polos* to destroy us." The catholic priests consider this ancestor obsession as analogous to the Christian veneration of saints while they ignore the Ngada's fear of *polos* as something non-existent.

However, in the last few years, the Ngada people have found a new confidence in their traditional rituals. Nonetheless, the Ngada continue to profess to be devout Christians. And just as well, Bahasa Indonesia is used for Catholic rites while traditional rituals that involve communicating with the ancestors and the *polos* are carried out in traditional Ngada dialects.

Ngada societies are matrilineal and the husbands stay with their wives after the wedding. This is more of a recent phenomenon because before colonisation by the Dutch, when the Ngada used to be warring societies, the powerful warriors followed a patriarchal system with brides taking residence in the groom's house. In those days, only the men without much social standing would follow the system that is in vogue now. But as wars between the tribes were controlled, only a few wealthy men could afford to follow the practice of staying at their own homes after marriage because social rules indicated that in such a situation, the bride's family had to be paid an exorbitant compensation. In this respect, the Ngada are quite similar to the Garo and Jaintia tribes of North-Eastern India.

All the same, the matrilineal and matrilocal systems haven't improved the lot of women in Ngada cultures. Like any society where household work is not monetised, Ngada women have to perform hard physical labour all day while having a limited say in the management of the villages or the ever-important rituals. Cooking, weaving, cleaning, giving birth and then tending to the children, bringing small things to within hand's reach of the ever squatting husband; these are the preoccupations of most of the women in these villages. On the other hand, many young husbands supposedly also live rather miserably, away from their childhood homes, bereft of a social support circle, conscious of their strangeness; problems typically faced by newly married brides in most societies. Often, they are made fun of in their new homes, their work criticised as their reputation takes time to build up. They are bullied by the wife's unmarried brothers who are still sharing the house, just like conventional sisters-in-law. But as they have children, and contribute to the work in the fields, they start gaining political power. But with many couples ending up with eight or more children and both their traditional religion and new found Catholicism encouraging this process, there is now less fertile land left for newly wed couples to start a livelihood from. Many of the men of Nage had therefore taken to working for others, as construction workers or manual labourers.

On the way back to Bajawa, Lobo got another scare when she and Roni skid off a rock and almost fell. As Roni and his brother began fixing the bent parts of Roni's bike, she sat down a bit far from them. Tears were rolling down her eyes because she thought she was within death's breath. The two brothers were also traumatised and when we took a stop at the hot river, they held each other and stood in the water to calm their nerves. The brothers, wearing oversized jackets and helmets, looking rather stiff, were in stark contrast to the boisterous naked boys who were still playing in the waters. Lobo was too shocked to risk anything and stayed away. We swapped our brothers and after the treacherous stretch of the road was over, they drove like professional racers with a point to prove. Now, it was my time to invite tears for Roni kept getting calls on his mobile. While speeding along the winding roads, he would check the number calling him with a quick glance and then insert the phone inside his helmet to fix it there. When we finally reached our hotel, the brothers finally let out their desperation. Roni was suffering from severe back and neck pain and he had many bleeding wounds on his legs. His brother seemed to be physically fine but looked at Roni with sorrowful eyes.

At night, we went back to meet Mama Mena and her sister. We had carried some gifts for them and in return, they packed us a lot of fruits. Till today, Mama Mena keeps messaging us, enquiring about our health and even calls us at times, spending her meagre income to help us remain connected to the wonderful memory of interacting with them. As for Roni and his brother, we hadn't got as close to them as we had to Emyl and Sil, but Roni too kept messaging me asking about our whereabouts all the time we were in Indonesia. Other than Emyl, Mama Mena and Roni, the only other people messaging me were those from my bank in Singapore, sending in tender messages asking me to buy their various products. In a foreign land, where no one spoke my mother tongue, I cherished these messages from someone who always seemed to think about what I may like or what I may need and spent money to let me know about it.

Where the water changes its clothes

The next day we headed for Ende, the second biggest town in Flores after Maumere. We booked a 'travel' again and this time our driver looked like Pele. For some reason, all van drivers in Flores look like Brazilian soccer stars. A middle-aged man, he immediately assumed the role of serving as our gracious uncle for the duration of the journey which, of course, was to be precisely four hours. The mist was very thick but as we came down from the hills of Bajawa, the weather cleared up slowly. We were glad to escape from the gloomy clouds that had been our constant companion for over a week. By the time, we caught a glimpse of the sea, the sun was out in full force reminding us that we were still very close to the equator.

The day after, we headed to the village of Moni, the usual base for visiting the Kelimutu lakes, the highlight of Flores. As expected, our bemo circled all around Ende looking for passengers and came back to our hotel twice in the process, leaving us wondering why we had bothered to hire ojeks to go to the bemo terminal. The heat and stuffiness inside the overcrowded van was made more bearable by the friendliness of the other passengers who offered us food and tried to shrink their bodies a bit more so that we would be comfortable. If only some of these friendly people knew that we could do without their smoking. That would have been difficult to expect in Indonesia, the smoking capital of the world. Indonesians also don't like to keep the windows open when smoking inside a van. As we were about to get smoked like eels, the views outside turned glorious. We were riding along the edges of a gorge sandwiched between vertical cliffs. Small rice fields had been carved out wherever there was a little flat space along the walls of the hills. We twisted our necks in all direction to catch a glimpse and observing that, our fellow passengers sacrificed their window seats to us so that we could enjoy better their beautiful country. We jumped at this opportunity to open the windows and escape from the cigarette onslaught. Sticking our necks out of the windows like rear view mirrors, we arrived at the tiny hamlet of Moni.

Moni is a very quiet place that only comes to life when bemos pass by dropping tourists. A clutch of hotels that look more like normal homes are scattered on both sides of the Trans Flores Highway, closely bordered by the hills. A handful of restaurants with hippy vibes wait numbly for customers. A tethered goat keeps jumping back and forth a drain. It happily accepts any blade of grass offered to it. In front of a rice field, a black pig noisily digs the ground to make a comfortable bed for itself. Nearby, a black piglet that appears like a 'before' version from the 'before-after' hair-loss advertisements, busily explored things on the ground. Its thin tail seemed to have a mind of its own, twirling uncontrollably.

The village was only half a kilometre in length and as the Trans Flores Highway left Moni, rice fields took over till the road met the horizon. After fierce negotiations with the different hotel owners, we settled for Hidaya homestay. The place had spacious rooms with cheerful green walls and peacock blue bed sheets over a Lobo-certified firm mattress. A honeymoon style mosquito net hung from the ceilings. It took us a few attempts to bundle up the loose hanging end of the net and throw it like a shot-put ball over the top base so that it doesn't divide the bed into India and China. Hidaya also happened to be located across the ant highway in Moni. Thick, succulent hordes of them carried unfortunate moths over their head like a mass funeral march.

It had been raining all week in Moni. When we arrived, it had stopped raining but the sky was completely blanketed in grey. There seemed to be little hope of viewing Kelimutu but I thought we could at least see something if we left then, around noon. The next day we could again go to the lakes for the more conventional sunrise view. Again, we chanced upon two brothers who agreed to take us to the peaks on their bikes.

Kelimutu was discovered only in 1915 by Dutch explorer Van Telen and its colour-changing attributes had to wait for another fifteen years to gain fame when a certain Mr. Bouman began writing profusely about it. The colours of the lakes had been different a few years back. Two of these lakes, that are turquoise now, had then been red and green. The change of colours is assumed to be owing to the changes in water levels brought about by rainfall, evaporation and seepage. With the changing water levels, different salts from the rocks dissolve in varying concentrations, thus giving the lakes a change of coating every few years. The changes of colours in Kelimutu are also not predictable. The last eruption at Kelimutu had occurred in 1968. The lakes are sixty to one hundred twenty metres deep and their diameter vary from three hundred fifty to four hundred metres. Their temperatures are different and while all three are usually around thirty degrees Celsius, at times, one lake was supposed to have crossed sixty. There is no evidence of life within the lakes.

As we climbed the hills, the mist got denser. Our brothers were driving by intuition hoping to hear rather than see any vehicle coming from the opposite direction. I could see small drops of water sticking to my eyelashes. Two French tourists were coming down and we asked them if they could see anything, "Nothing, we could see nothing," theycomplained in utter desperation. But all of a sudden, after we crossed the park entrance, the sky started clearing up, as if the weather waited for the fees. Bit by bit, as we climbed higher, we could see more around us. Both Lobo and I kept looking at the sky. There I could see a small patch of blue; then again, I could clearly see some of the trees that surrounded us; soon the first rays of sunlight hit my face and I looked up in sheer delight. Once we alighted, Lobo came running to me and said that she had been cheering the sun. We ran to the lakes like two kids chasing the last remaining packet of candy in the world.

Our ojek brothers stayed behind, perhaps bored of the views of Kelimutu, or perhaps considerate to give us the benefit of solitude at one of the omnipresent calendar icons of Flores. A few stray chickens scampered for cover as we jumped over puddles on the way to the lake. The sun kept trying its best to sweep out the mess in the sky and when we arrived at the first lake, there was just a candyfloss-sized lump of cloud reluctantly climbing up and out of the crater. From the viewing point, guarded by an annoying red railing, we saw the swimming pool-sized turquoise lake, a little unimpressive for its reputation. But we were exhilarated more at the fortunate turn of events which had made it possible. Restless, we bumped into every inch of the railing, to catch a view from all angles, like two people trying to get rid of ice slipped through the neck of their clothes.

Tucked just above one corner of the lake, was the second one, another turquoise sliver of a water body from that viewing point. Scraggy and lifeless brick coloured rocky walls enclosed the lakes. We left the two lakes to rush to the highest point from where all the three lakes would be visible, afraid that the sun would set soon. Wide steps led the way to the top on which a curious pillar had been erected. We tripped a few times along the way as we kept looking back at the two lakes we had just left behind. From some illusion of vision, the first lake now appeared to be higher than the second; the size of the two lakes had also reversed. Once we reached the top, the third lake was visible, located opposite the first two lakes, with the viewing platform and the conspicuous pillar in between. The third lake is a few notches more mysterious than the first two, albeit the same size as both. The steep crater walls enclosing this Coke-coloured lake had vines climbing in from the crater rim while the sun glared from behind its walls, making it difficult to keep looking at the lake for long. The lake was now alive and held the position of power in what must be a rotating arrangement among the three, determined by the movement of the sky around the sun. The taxman Pedor, whom we had met on the bemo from Labuan Bajo to Ruteng, had told us that it was possible to drink from the Coke coloured lake but the crater walls were too steep for us to consider a sip

The real beauty of Kelimutu lies in its mysteriously interrupted silence. With no one else around, when we shut our mouth and stopped congratulating ourselves on our foresight and daredevil travel planning, the silence of the place, alive and encroaching, enveloped us. When we listened to this silence, we heard the roar of an army of wind approaching from an unknown direction, reminding us of childhood stories of young girls walking alone in the woods. Muffled explosions were happening somewhere from time to time, perhaps within these lakes. Something went inside the turquoise lake but we missed it. Ripples, here and there; what life breathed inside these buckets?

Something came up perhaps, again from one of the turquoise lakes. Behind their walls, someone was pulling over a massive blanket of white clouds.

Over sixteen hundred metres above sea level, the weather at Kelimutu changes frequently during the course of the day. A pall of mist passed over us and we felt each needlepoint of moisture, twinkling in the sunlight. A sliver of a rainbow appeared from nowhere and as if it was already not enough to satisfy us, halos appeared over our shadows. Giant shadows also moved around back and forth and the lakes underneath them gained new shapes with them. Their colours changed with the fading light and we were tempted to say "I love you" to each other in praise of a beautiful timeless universe.

For the people living in the surroundings, the word Kelimutu means boiling lake. The Coke-coloured lake is called Tiwu Ata Mbupu that stands for 'lake of the elders'. One of the turquoise lakes was called Tiwu Nua Muri Koohi Fah, meaning the lake for young men and maidens, while the first lake as the visitors arrive from the park entrance is called Tiwu Ata Polo, the lake of evil spirits. Scientists call them by the acronyms TAM, TiN and TAP. The local Lio tribe believe that after death, the spirits of the people who died at old age go to reside at TAM, those who died young go to TiN, and the spirits of those who happened to be evil spirited in their lifetime take shelter at TAP. TAP didn't seem to be a worse place than either TAM or TiN except for being bordered by that ugly red railing. Before the spirit or *mae* took shelter in these lakes, he or she had to meet the guardian at the gates called *Konde Ratu* who would then assign them their eternal home. Nonetheless, as shelters for the dead, all these small lakes must be extremely crowded spaces and the upwellings in these lakes were testimonial to the constant jostling and shuffling that must have been taking place inside.

Every year, on August 14th, during the festival of *Pati ka dua bapu ata mata*, hundreds of Lio people went to these lakes to make food offerings and seek blessings from the resident ancestors. These used to be bloody rituals with sacrifices of large animals but the practice was stopped about fifty years ago under pressure from the Catholic Church. For now, it was hard to tell how the ancestors took to this development because even though the Lio believe that lakes change colours with the changing moods of the ancestors, the lack of any definite pattern gave a confused understanding of their situation. Later I came to know that the locals also believe that visitors hoping to get a clear morning sky on their day of visiting Kelimutu should bring small gifts for *Konde Ratu*. It was evident that no one had bothered to do this over the last week.

When we reluctantly headed back to the park entrance, a few old people were waiting for us. They were from the dozen rickety shops, each standing on four poles, at both sides of the park entrance. It was getting dark but they were hoping we would buy something from them in what must have been a miserable week. All we could think of buying from them were two bottles of water. The ojek brothers were quite excited and gave us high fives on our luck with Kelimutu. In our rush when we had left Moni for Kelimutu, I didn't get much of a chance to engage with them and only now, I realised that the two brothers looked strikingly different from one another. The elder brother, Gus, had more of Javanese features with deep furrows in the hairless cheeks, short straight hair and brown skin. The younger one, Fred, had a huge afro, was of much darker complexion, and sported a goatee. Both, however, seemed to be of the exact same height. As we climbed down from Kelimutu, the clouds rolled back in. Rather quickly, it became completely dark and again the ojek brothers had to navigate the road relying on their ears.

We made a stop at the hot springs just before Moni. In the darkness, Fred used his mobile phone to light the way. It was unpaved and had become very muddy from the rain. We came across a handful of houses and from one of them, a young girl came out to ask us the entry price of five thousand rupiah or fifty cents. The hot springs pool was the outcome of the entrepreneurial spirit of her family. At the back of their house, they had built two tiled pools where they channelled the hot waters from Kelimutu, one for each sex. The ladies' pool was built a step below the men's pool. In the dark, we just dumped our clothes on the steps leading to the pools, and then lumped them together for some sense of security from theft. Loud and happy chatter was coming out of both the pools. The patrons had converted the idea of hot springs to more of a bathing place as the water seemed to be full of soap suds and shampoo lather. Many men were washing their huge afros. In the darkness, only their lion silhouettes were visible. The water was pleasantly warm and in the light drizzle, we became lazy turtles gawking at the outlines of trees in the shadow of the night.

Back at Moni, we had the best food we had had so far in Indonesia at our hotel restaurant. The owner, a cousin of the ojek brothers, explained that they had gone to Maumere to get the Indian spices that made their food special. The curries we had ordered were indeed Indian in name and spirit, but tasted quite different yet delicious. Timeless backpacking classics by Deep Purple, Rainbow and Guns'n'Roses were playing and a few afro-haired young men had assembled. Fred was also there and serving us food while Gus sat down with us. He had been married for over seven years and had three daughters. "I had an afro like Gus as well. In our culture, we have to cut it before marriage and become a good boy from then," he said. Then he came closer and whispered in my ears, "Fred has a girlfriend in Germany. He wants to go there. But she has not been kind enough yet."

Across the other table, a chubby man with a smaller afro began talking to us. His name was Mateo Gaton and he was accompanying an all-women tourist group from Germany as their driver and guide. He spoke English fluently and had a fire in his eyes, "You are not visiting so many wonderful parts of Flores. Have you heard of the whale hunting festival in Lamarella near Larantuka? The entire village comes to the shores to see off the whalers. They only have small harpoons. They go in small wooden boats before sunrise. The man with the harpoon jumps on to the whale with the harpoon. He can be killed, you know? Waaa!" When we asked him where he lived, he said, "I don't need a home. I am always in my car, today in Ende, tomorrow in Moni, the day after in Riung. This is my home"

The only other tourists in Moni, a father-son duo from France, came to the restaurant. Earlier, we had seen them coming back from Kelimutu. To rub it in, I asked them if they could see the lakes and that we had seen it all. They shrugged their shoulders. The locals present in the restaurant asked them to go again the next day but they said that they had waited enough and would go to Bajawa the next day. The locals went on trying to persuade them, and to silence them, the son assured them, "Yeah, yeah, next year, next year."

That night, we walked around the dark streets of Moni up and down a few times, hoping to catch more people to boast about our luck with Kelimutu. But we couldn't find any more tourists and it was not fun boasting to the local people who may have seen the lakes several times in its various moods. Nonetheless, many of the families were sitting and chatting idly outside their homes and as we crossed each house, they all called out to enquire about us and congratulate us for they all seemed to know that we had been lucky with Kelimutu.

We went inside a dimly lit shop where a Ronnie James Dio look-alike, with a balding forehead, but long afro beyond that, was comforting a black puppy. He told us that the mother of the puppy had been killed in a road accident the day before, something he said was very common in Flores. They called the puppy Manis or sweet. The father dog came in as well, looking tender and sorrowful. He was called Papa Manis, renamed after his more illustrious son. But Dio said that he had already found a new wife, hearing which Lobo gave him the benefit of doubt saying it was only to arrange for milk for the puppy. The new wife followed in soon but looked disinterested about the puppy.

I began talking to the man managing the store, an old man who spoke with a lisp and deference that came easily to people from this region when they first encounter foreigners. He didn't own the store himself but only worked there as a hired hand. Since he lived two kilometres away from Moni, at the village with the hot springs, he stayed over every night at the shop and went back to his village only during weekends. Working as a hired hand in a shop that was itself far from any sign of prosperity; another familiar life story in Flores.

We had missed making offerings to *Konde Ratu* and the next morning, it was raining cats and dogs, spoiling any hope of catching the sunrise at Kelimutu, an event always featuring in the Flores top ten. We had set our alarms before sunrise and they rang regardless of the weather outside. When we woke up, we had little desire to go out in such weather. But we had asked the two ojek brothers to pick us up. I messaged Fred asking him to cancel the trip but he didn't message back. Assured that the brothers were fast asleep, we slept our way through.

The bemo from Moni to Ende was crowded and smoke-filled as expected. Only half of my bum was resting on a seat. But we forgot all the discomfort as we anxiously kept watch on a cow standing on the van we were following along the way. As the van swooped left and right along the winding highway, its knees wobbled and it struggled to keep balance. Many times we gasped as it almost fell over the railings. Our fellow passengers were also glued to this spectacle and cheered the cow along with us. We all knew its eventual fate in the slaughterhouse but just didn't want it to die yet. It got some respite when we were stuck at a road repair point where traffic came to a standstill. Our driver shared his cigarette with the construction workers who were moving from bemo to bemo, taking one puff at each stop. The cow looked at them with curiosity and sat down for the first time.

Facing the border of two worlds

Ende, the second biggest town in Flores after Maumere, had an air of confidence about itself. It was indeed the big boy of Flores. The shoulders of the people looked stronger. Young men sported spiky hairdos that were coloured blonde or blue. Women walked fast with their heads held high. This was not a place for shy giggles when one saw a stranger. People of the streets would scream out a "hello" to draw our attention and then quickly follow up with a confident "goodbye". At the same time, it has the genuine warmth of a cosmopolitan city that was not isolated but also not a tourist destination. There was a frenzy of activities and movements along its broad streets, very unlike the other towns of Flores. Much of the town was located along the coast and from its borders, mountains, some of them volcanoes, climbed steeply. Along this coast, many things happened in Ende.

We walked along the coast from the west; our first stop was the Ende Maritime Museum, a small setup, little more than a dark room where many specimens were kept in the glass cupboards lining the walls, and a large showcase in the centre. There were fish bones, giant mollusc shells, turtle shells, and coral remains inside but only a fortunate few had labels. A whale's rib cage and its jaw bone was kept on the floor. Moore bones and shells were scattered on the floor. The highlight of the museum was the only person working there, a small young man who filled in many roles, security guard, ticketing agent, guide, gardener, and also the cleaner. We were the only visitors and from the guestbook, it appeared that it had been a while since the last visitors had come. The humble museum had humble entry fees which our multi-talented man collected with all humility. With folded hands, he showed us around the specimens. He took special pride in talking to us about the bones of the whale (*ikan paus*) and the dolphins (*lumba-lumba*). Everything in that museum came from along the coast of Ende. But along all these specimens of death, this museum was somehow a favourite haunt of mosquitoes. Our young man kept slapping himself frenetically as he explained to us the mysterious creatures of the sea. We too kept slapping ourselves in matching beats as we listened to him in awe. He was delighted when we showed interest in anything and we feigned the expression of being amazed at every item he had to show. If only the government had provided him with mosquito repellents, he would have gained the fame of David Attenborough.

Next to the museum, there was a huge playground on one side of the road. Young boys, perhaps less than ten years old, were playing soccer. We began watching the boys' soccer but the kids left their game to come and talk to us. When we asked their names, they said Messi, Ronaldo, Maradona, Pele, Socrates. The young brats began asking Lobo for kisses and we had to hurry to rescue Lobo.

As we kept walking towards the east, along the coast, we passed by the Pelni harbour. After the harbour, a row of ikat shops followed. Here we met Iskander, the conqueror of the world, and the greatest salesman ever whom Arthur Miller would have loved to meet. We found him gossiping with the owner of the first ikat stall along the way. Strangely, he took us around all the other open ikat shops before bringing us to his own. He appeared to be very knowledgeable and went into a rolling description about the origins and customs associated with ikat. Alas, he didn't have a mirror. So he hunted around for a long time and came back with a *cermin*, or mirror, that clearly was a small broken fragment from a larger mirror. But his big smile erased any suspicion of mirror sabotage. He clapped as Lobo and I tried one piece after another saying, "Better, even better!" with each new trial. Lobo was worried that in his enthusiasm, he might clap forcefully with the broken mirror still in his hand.

The ikat shops get more organised with better décor as one keeps moving west, which means that they use glass cupboards and mannequins instead of displaying the clothes on tree branches and discarded cement blocks. But Ende, if not the whole world, can only have one Iskander, and without him, these more glamorous shops seemed little more than faceless warehouses. May he be spared by the malarial mosquitoes that felled Alexander the Great.

We moved on and smells began to embrace us; smells of death and decay, recent and a little more recent, of just slaughtered animals and fish, of fish already dried neatly into crusty heaps, a giant drum full of severed buffalo heads, their eyes still brooding, surrounded by a garden of rotting discarded vegetable parts. We were in Pasar Ende, the main market, and we were surrounded by a criss-cross of frenzied movements, ojeks making their way like a family of gigantic metal ants, porters rushing with their springy feet, shouting for their right of way, children jumping over red and green chillies arranged in neat circles by the old ladies who had encroached upon the muddy road. It was a surreal forest of vegetables without their trees and animals without their hides and heads; nature living perfectly in harmony with humans. Police screamed on megaphones to keep order and asked pick-pockets to go home and rest for the day.

The Pasar reached its glory at its eastern end, the Pasar Ikan, or fish market. About a dozen vendors sat on stilted platforms on both sides of a narrow alley connecting Ende with the sea that opened out into the beach where the catch was brought in and auctioned. Giant yellow fin tuna lay on these stilted shops in a timeless manner. At some shops, there were only lonely cut sections, hinting of the greatness of the fish that it belonged to, the fish that had lived in utter disregard of the land and its dwellers all its life. Lonely too, in death, was a very colourful fish, surrounded by the death all around in shades of grey. Neat heaps of small fish had been arranged by some of the men, with an arched fish on their top like cake icing, almost looking happy and frolicking in permanence. The stench and death of this place must have appeared very unbearable and shocking if there was nothing else at that place but the dead fish, an omen of something dreadful that is approaching. But there were the sellers and the buyers who made the place look normal, even pleasant, with their warm smiles, gentle eyes, and humble voices, some asking about us, some explaining the fish they had put on display and others telling us about their lives. Two old men with broken teeth began talking, "We come very early in the morning. Then we can get a better bargain from the fishermen. They are tired then after a whole night out in the sea. By midday, no one comes here. We leave then to sell the fish to the restaurants." *"Lihat raja saya",* screamed a man from behind, asking us to look at his king, an unusual yellow fish with a giant head on a disproportionately small body. Its mouth was open with an unfinished command. Two dolphins lay in neglect, with only the front halves of their bodies. Their eyes were unusually small and sad unlike the fish. Their skin was smooth like rubber and their long snouts had hundreds of teeth like small kerbstones. It seemed like they had been executed. Perhaps they had been mother and child, which one died first and did the other see it die?

At the beach, the auctions were still going on. Young boys, some naked, were ferrying in small boats to bring the catch in buckets from the bigger wooden boats anchored a few metres from the shore. These boys looked very focused, perhaps pretending to be more worldly-wise than they really were to show off against those studious boys from town who had come along with their fathers, just to have a look. Two men brought on shore a giant manta ray, holding it by its fins. They dumped it on the sand like Hector. A crowd soon gathered around it. The crowd pushed us to the front to take pictures. Some asked us to touch its mouth. It was soft like grandfather's gums. After some time, Achilles came. He looked young and strong. One of the carriers of the manta handed him a machete. He stood over the ray, his legs spread apart, and then holding the machete, pointed his finger at all of us, "Give me a darn good price!" Everyone was too shy and awed by his stance. When a bunch of scrawny old men grouped up to make a hesitant offer, Achilles hurled a volley of praises about the great qualities of Hector and what it took to slay him, "He fought all night. Look how big it is! Are you crazy?" But perhaps he was just waiting to say this, because despite his violent instant rejection of the asking price, he instantly obliged. Hector was chopped into fine pieces and dispatched. The crowd dispersed and we lost Achilles.

Similar auctions were happening at many places as the boats kept coming from their nightly sojourns. The shore was the border where the people of Ende exhibited the spoils of the battles they fought every night riding on the upwelling of the Sawu Sea. Sawu Sea was named after the tiny island of Sawu that was to the south of Flores. Sumatra didn't get a sea named after it, neither did Kalimantan, Sumbawa or Lombok. But little Sawu had a sea. People change names of roads, towns, and countries at their whims. But names of seas hardly change. The only possibility is the South China Sea which the Filipinos may someday get everyone to call as the West Philippines Sea. As for the Sawu sea, the future of its name looks safe.

The action at the shores died down soon and everyone left to allow the boats to rest in their cradle, the Sawu Sea. The place came alive again in the evening when the gangs of Ende took over the place. These gangs comprised of boys of all ages, some perhaps only five years old. Like a bunch of monkeys tending to each other, the younger ones sucked up to the leaders by helping them to apply hair gel and then painting their hair in shades of white, gold or even blue. After decorating their masters, the youngest boys would take off their clothes, stand in a line, run towards the sea, and jump into it with somersaults. They did this many times while the older boys looked on. We cheered the young ones on and this made the kids try to leap higher and further. Some fell awkwardly and were greeted with laughter. They asked us to cheer them more while the older boys were disengaged from us. Once tired, these young acrobats rolled about in the black sand and then took one final shower before packing up. The youngest of them all came up to us and giggled, "Money." One of the older boys came up to him, caught him in an arm-grip, demobilised him and pushed him into the sand. After that, they left one by one, looking ready for the night.

Further east to the Pasar Ikan, there are a series of big all-purpose stores run by people of Chinese origin. They all sell the same goods, a haberdashery of things from small orange juice bottles to medicines for curing erection problems. All of them look the same. That stretch of the city ended in two sparkling white mosques made in Arabic style.

As we turned back, we came across a Chinese-owned restaurant which was gloriously written about in travel guides. The menu was expensive and big plastic lobsters and crabs looked over us from all corners. A Chinese man came to take our order and once he saw me he said, "*Lihat!*" or "Watch" and then danced as he sung one line from an Indian film song, *Kuch kuch hota hai*. Lobo was utterly distressed by the food like any Northern Chinese person is when she comes in contact with food from the Southern Chinese Coasts. She complained that they never knew what to do with vegetables and so just boiled them up. She bemoaned that their hot plate tofu could have just as well been called the thunder plate, holding up to heavens an offering of tomato sauce. When the bill came, she was livid and promised never to try Chinese food again in Indonesia and the other one hundred and ninety one members of the United Nations bar China.

At the other end of the town, at the intercity bemo terminal, it's a rare arena for aggression in Indonesia. Agents of the local bemos will dash in the moment a bemo arrives from another city. They try to get the attention of the passengers by screaming. What stops them from pulling passengers by hands is the pull on their own hands by the other agents. From where the passenger sits, all he could see is a bunch of screaming heads arranged in a floral pattern, each one's collar or neck grabbed by another hand.

Ende has a longer formal history than the rest of Flores. It had long been a settling ground for conflicts. Two of the volcanoes at Ende, Pui and

Iya, had fought bitterly for centuries before Iya had cut off Pui's head with a big knife. As a result, Pui now looks like a miniature of the Table Mountain of Cape Town. A big rock jutting out from the sea is said to be Pui's head, still awaiting a burial. The small island of Pulau Ende, about two hundred metres from the shore of Ende, is the knife that Iya had used. Taking a cue from these mountains, Ende was also used as the battleground to settle scores by the Portuguese who came in from their base in Solor, the Muslim traders from Java during the sixteenth century, and the Dutch from the seventeenth.

The Portuguese had built fortresses in and around Ende. In one legend, Rendo, the daughter of the Portuguese commander, had a Javanese lover, Jebe, who also worked as a servant in the fortress of Ende. The Javanese pirates attacked the fortress and killed Jebe while Rendo's father was away. Rendo was famous for her beauty and the pirates searched all over the fortress for her. She and her maid managed to get hold of a fishing boat and set sail. Livid, the leader of the pirates prayed for storms and the heavens obliged. Rendo and her maid died in the sea and a princely state was established in Ende.

While the Dutch conquered much of Flores over the next hundred years, they entered into a contract with the Muslim rulers of Ende. This contract was intact until 1907 when the Dutch colonial government established complete control and made Ende their capital in Flores. The villages around Ende fought the Dutch during this period, led by Mari Longa. As a young boy, Mari Longa had been rather sickly. His father changed his name from the one given after his birth, Leba, to Mari Longa, a tree with bitter skin and hard wood. Mari Longa's health improved immediately. After Ende had been ransacked by his army of villagers bearing arrows and swords, the Dutch sent in their forces and Mari Longa was killed. Today, a road in Ende has been named after him and a big statue of Mari Longa stands, rather provocatively, at a major crossroad.

A tree in Ende also played a key role in Indonesia's history. Next to the playground, where we were bullied by the young boys asking for kisses, stands a breadfruit tree under which Sukarno, the first president of free Indonesia, had come up with his ideas of Pancasila, or five principles, for governing Indonesia. The Pancasila principles, in some modified form, had also formed the basis for the pointless Non-Aligned Movement. The inspiring tree, however, is a replacement, because the original had been uprooted by a storm.

The effect of this history of Ende is visible in its cosmopolitan population. The city is distinctly more Javanese than Florenese although sixty per cent of the people follow Christianity, the rest following Islam. There is a considerable population of people with Chinese, Arab and Indian origins. The Caucasian influence remains largely in the architecture of the churches. The people living outside the city limits, in the several small villages, are the Lio people. Given the nature of Ende's interactions with the outside world, the culture and customs of the Lio people have probably dissolved at a faster rate than the rest of Flores. While a few traditional villages exist, they are now mostly an amalgamation of randomly scattered modern houses with only one or two traditional houses remaining.

We headed towards the weaving villages of Ndona in a half-hearted search for this tradition. This time, our ojek drivers were not brothers as far as they knew. The village was well prepared for tourists though none were heading for it. Children returning from school ran in all directions as soon as they saw us, screaming, "Tourist! Tourist! *Orang Asing*," or foreigners! Hearing the call, women, old and older, came out, some half-dressed, having barely got much time to prepare for our arrival. They ambushed us holding ikats to their bosoms. Scared, our ojek drivers stopped immediately and left us on our own. The ladies began waving their ikats at us like matadors. We looked at all direction like hapless bulls but restrained our urge to charge. Seeing our inaction, some old women took things under their control, and pulled Lobo, and myself along with her, inside one of the houses. The men of the house ran out and in the darkness, one lady pulled our hands to display an old woman squatting in front of us to show how the weaving happens. That two second demonstration was supposed to have warmed us up and a gang of women surrounded us to get us buy the ikats. Even if we had wanted to buy anything, none were attractive, and with our hands moving like frenetic car window wipers, we pushed our way out of this ikat cave. We ran for our ojek drivers, who had very sensibly positioned themselves for just an eventuality like this. We sped past the village which could have been called from now on, 'Another Village of Bitter Ikat Women'.

There is something about ikat weaving that makes the weaver restless. We had experienced this in all parts of Indonesia. While the ikat traders and middlemen remain rather sanguine about the prospects of selling their ikat, the weavers themselves become desperate and bitter when someone refuses to buy them. The weaving process is tiring and the final output none too extraordinary. At the same time, the occasional demand for ikat in the west as ethnographic objects, often in bulk quantities, gives a misperception that every visitor is an ethnographer.

So the ikat weavers, those poor women, when they come face to face with a visitor, at first believe whole-heartedly that the ikat is the only object missing in the visitor's pampered vacuous life. These weavers are assured that the moment the visitor's eyes fall on the ikat they are holding, the visitor would scream, "I want that one, and that one, and that one too", and then collapse in ecstasy. But when the visitor doesn't behave like this and the weavers notice the first sign of disinterest, they become sceptical, of their own work, and the tourist's interpretation of the meaning of life. They turn sceptical about the whole world and soon become hysterical. Some pull the tourist while some chase after them. The best behaved merely present a facial expression that dismisses the tourist as a lowly creature, lower than the lizards and frogs they had weaved in the clothes that belonged rather well to a gone past.

Escaping from Ndona, we headed for the village for Wolotopo. The road bordered the sea, at places climbing over hills and squeezing in between them, giant rocks precariously hanging on top. Such drives should have been considered breathtaking but was becoming a habit for us in Flores. We were complaining that the skies were too cloudy and the sea of Ende was therefore not as blue as we would have liked to have.

The village of Wolotopo rose steeply from the sea and had a *favela*-like feel to it, without the drug lords. A couple of traditional houses were still standing in full glory, surrounded by the modern concrete cube houses, painted in pastel colours, pink and yellow being the most favoured. The two traditional houses were considerably bigger than what we had encountered so far. They were similar to the Ngade houses in their defined edges and corners and the huge shaggy rooftops. But as they were built on the slope, they had a much bigger platform at their base, made out of brick-sized rocks. This gave these houses a fortress-like appearance to the waist, about five metres high, followed by the wooden walls and the giant roof made of *alang-alang*. From a distance, it was easy to compare it with an unruly grandmother wearing a pebble skirt.

We were yet to master how to behave in a traditional village. Shy, surrounded by glances, we would hesitantly head for the kids, offering them the stickers. It worked as always, the news spread and more kids came to us, sometimes accompanied by their fathers, mothers or elder sisters, who would engage us in some *obrol*. A big group started following us as we roamed around the village but soon dispersed as they lost interest. We were only left with a bunch of children who had just come back from school. They laughed as they saw us trying to feed goats with grass and offered us to join in a game of banging a tin drum. Once we grew bored with them and headed towards our ojek, the older among these children continued to follow us and when the engines started and we set off, one of them made an unsuccessful attempt to touch Lobo.

We headed to the village of Nangapanda, known for its shore full of coloured stones. It was a long stretch of smooth pebbles and rocks that came in shades of blue, purple, green, white and black. One of the ojek drivers, Rushtom, joined us as we set about collecting the smaller pieces. A few women were also squatting and collecting the bigger rocks in buckets. These women made six thousand rupiah for each bucket, combing the shore each day. These stones were then exported to Japan for their famed rock gardens. It must have been quite a journey for these rocks, coming up from depths of the sea, perhaps sometimes licked by the gooey drips of sea creatures, then on to the shore, burned by the sun and slapped by the waves, picked up by poor hands of misfortune, finally resting in the eyes of a Zen follower in a sparse Kyoto garden.

We were collecting smaller shards and some sea glass to decorate our small turtle bowl back in Singapore. Rushtom made his own judgements about where our interests lay and began to pick big stones on our behalf. To avoid offending him, we would take these with an expression of wonder, with unspoken plans of throwing them back in Ende. My bag became ridiculously heavy in the process. On one big rock, we saw a blue jelly fish left behind by the tide. It was puffing, looking like an air-blown blue condom, moving its head in all directions for the vagina that had left it behind to die.

Once back in Ende, we walked the streets again. While little remains of the Portuguese forts in Ende, today the modern city has a big army garrison, right next to the Maritime Museum. Young men, considerably taller and stronger than the locals, walked inside in small groups in their camouflage uniforms. When we passed them by, a few enthusiastic men, who were taking down the flag, called out to us, "Good evening, How are you?" We spoke back in Bahasa Indonesia but they insisted in conversing in broken English.

Our search for good food continued in vain. Satays fresh from the grill were remarkably cold and dumplings evolved into strange dollops. Even at Hotel Ikhlas, whose fish and chips were glorified in some travel books as the best thing the Orient had produced drawing inspiration from British culture, our disappointment was unanimous. It is always a pleasure to prove travel guides wrong, a kind of feeling one gets when one hears the news of an investment bank making huge losses. Nonetheless, Hotel Ikhlas had charms of its own. Run by a family with mixed Indian and Arab roots, it was one of the cheapest in Ende with the firmest bed. The hotel was perhaps patronised by the IPU or the Invisible Pink Unicorn, the omnipotent God of atheists. His painting adorned the bathroom door, with dreamy eyes, bordering between that of a rapist and a sage. Like most hotels in Flores, Ikhlas too was either designed too well for loving couples or not really designed for them. There would always be two small beds separated by a chasm that encouraged honeymooners to cuddle in real tight or give up love for the sake of comfort and sleep separately.

At the hotel, we met Luke, a British chef who was still recovering from goosebumps, having trekked some of the volcanoes of Indonesia. "My original purpose to come to Eastern Indonesia was to sample the cuisines and get some inspiration for my kitchen back home." But despite being British, he had American optimism. "Everywhere, I have only come across Masakan Padang or Southern Chinese food. Well, I am really looking forward to going to Bali soon where I hope that it will be better." We understood the pain of an avant-garde chef stuck in Flores and wished him all the best.

One night at Ende, we met up with Pak Banggo to teach English at his class. Before this, I took on the enormous task of shaving off my three-week-old beard. Initially, it had been days of pure happiness, a razor-free idyll. It had taken some convincing for Lobo to accept the beard. I gave all sorts of reasons; that it would save me from ultraviolet rays, project a Texas-like "don't mess with me" feel that would ward off prying eyes from her, and above all, make me look like the Chinese intellectuals idolised by Lobo. As the beard grew and grew, Lobo bought in to each of these arguments. But then the itch struck me and I began transforming into a cat, scratching more and more vigorously as days went by. I recalled the plight of my goldfish, which had once perished from an itch. It had swum round and round for days in the round bowl looking for a corner to scratch itself, eventually passing on the disease to other goldfish in the bowl who followed suit. But now, Lobo objected to cutting off the beard. She had already established in her mind my image as a Chinese intellectual and warned me of unforeseen circumstances if I forsook my only proof of claim to wisdom. I argued that the children in Pak Banggo's class might not be very receptive to me if I looked like a *kara* or giant ape. She obliged reluctantly. When I shaved it off, I looked at the messy horror film tangle floating on the basin, a bunch of squatters with a penchant for prime real estate.

Looking like a shorn alpaca, I joined Lobo to Pak Banggo's school in the evening. Pak Banggo was chubby with a perfectly spherical head and bright eyes. He had spent many of his years as a cook in Bali and then in a cruise ship and had travelled to many countries. Once he reached fifty, he had come back to Flores to work as an English teacher at an Ende school. He also gave private English lessons from a converted garage. The garage forced him to think like a swashbuckling entrepreneur, like all garages do. So he was always considering many new business ventures, his current bright idea being to rent out bicycles for tourists.

When we reached his place, the class was yet to begin. The students who had come were extremely shy. They huddled in one corner and giggled like a bunch of hamsters keeping close to stay warm. Pak Banggo asked them to transform into humans and greet us one by one and take our blessings by touching our feet. The students queued up and once they reached us, lost control of their limbs and collapsed at our feet. We rescued them one by one and put them into their seats. About fifteen had turned up that day, aged between five and fifteen. Half of them were girls. The boys, as usual, were shyer than the girls. Pak Banggo was a proud father and brought his seven-year-old son forward, "He is the smartest of them all. Come on, ask these visitors some questions. Show them how well you can speak." The boy hid his face behind his hands.

"Too shy, too shy, *Malu malu kucing*," screamed Pak Banggo. "What is *malu malu kucing* in English?" he asked the class.

We all answered in chorus, "Shy, shy cat."

Pak Banggo picked the topic for discussion that day; his trip once upon a time to Norway. He said he had seen ice and mountains and fish and ships. The class noted down the English words for these. Next, we discussed Pak Banggo's trip to New York where he had seen buildings and crowded streets and yellow taxis. The class noted down the English words for these as well. In Indonesia, where people naturally sought to merge with their shadows in shyness, Pak Banggo was unique. His bald head was always shining. We watched a video in English and it was our turn to explain it. I was a fish out of water as I struggled to make the children understand. I got lost for words, looked all around me, used arcane terms, and often moved on without checking if the giggling kids followed anything.

For long, I had held the dream of opening Free Schools, in line with the ideas of the Spanish radical Francisco Ferrer, to spread rationality and utopian ideals like wildfire among the masses. Out there, I was struggling to teach them how to have a basic conversation with an anglophone. The revolution was falling apart.

Lobo took over and despite having a much weaker grasp of Bahasa Indonesia than me, managed to engage the class with her natural warmth of gestures and tone. The class laughed and fell apart as Lobo compared my hirsute arms to that of a monkey. The revolution was saved.

The class ended too soon and the students again lined up to shake our hands and wish us a happy journey. Many pictures were taken, especially by the teenage girls. They all wanted to have their pictures taken with Lobo with their camera phones. Each one was paying about twenty dollars a month for this. Curiously, Pak Banggo didn't speak English that well himself. But once the children left, he explained to us the main purpose of his class, "I want them to be bold. They are too shy. They can only think of Ende and Flores. They need to think bigger. That's why I keep talking about my foreign trips. I don't want them to only think of becoming a teacher or a policeman in Ende." He wanted to tell the kids what Gandhi told, "My life is my message." His eyes shone as brightly as his forehead at that moment. My saturated mind, conditioned by years of exposure to American self-help talk, failed to appreciate this much so when he offered to take us out for dinner, we wriggled out of it with the million-year-old excuse of having some other plans already.

Our stay at Flores was coming to an end with Ende. We had met a long list of characters along the way, the ojek brothers at various towns, Mama Mena and the fruit sellers of Bajawa, Brazilian soccer stars doubling up as bemo drivers, and starving foreign chefs looking for that elusive culinary fix. But Flores had been more about getting licked by the forked tongue of nature; by the untrustworthy stare of the komodos; the slow approach of the zen cuttlefish; the coloured lakes of Kelimutu with their upwelling from resident dead spirits; the misty hills with silent horses of Wao Muda; the cut bodies of the dolphin mother and her child, the sea, ever changing its mood with the sun and the wind, holding gigantic books of mysteries within its depths; and the stars, stars and more stars, sitting at a safe distance to watch this all from some fixed perspective, embracing each other playfully only at night on the surface of a gently swaying sea, unaware of our two pairs of eyes watching them mesmerised, nonchalantly passing away precious moments from their ephemeral life.

Racing against the flying fish

It was the time to be sea-borne, a great journey, across the Sawu Sea from the island of Flores to Sumba. I had been very excited about this part of the journey, somewhere in my mind comparing myself with Magellan or Columbus. Of course, I was going to travel only one hundred and seventy kilometres, across waters charted thousands of times. But for a long time, I had created in my mind a sense of danger and adventure around this trip. I imagined that I would be huddled in a packed ramshackle boat rocked by tempestuous seas. Many times, I would recall stories of ferries sinking of the coast of Indonesia; sometimes because of weather; sometimes colliding with big cargo ships, unable to get away from its pull; and sometimes falling under its own weight. Perhaps, more than becoming a Magellan, I was hoping to tell the tale of having taken the Titanic and coming alive out of it.

Unfortunately, ferry accidents are indeed common in Indonesia. Ferries and ships are a part of life for this archipelago nation. Many Indonesians make a living in islands far from where their families are, and especially for the poor, ferries are the only means to unite again. Even for the rich, ferries may be the only reasonable way to travel between two adjacent islands because travelling by plane would mean going in the opposite direction for a distance of half the nation, to Bali or Jakarta, to catch a crazy connecting flight. Anyway, airplane accidents are also relatively common in Indonesia. This importance of the sea-route gives these ships and ferries a status of importance, like giant metal dragons, roaming the sea from island to island. So outside the major cities of Indonesia, these ships and ferries capture the imagination of all the locals.

There were two options to travel between Flores and Sumba. We could either take one of the big ships of Pelni, the national shipping company, or we could take several of the smaller ferries, the ones usually suffering from the occasional mishaps. Pelni is quite particular about these differences, about their size and safety record. When I had asked at the Pelni counter if they had any ferry to Sumba, the official courteously replied, "We don't have ferries. For ferries, you have to look somewhere else. We only have ships." Only upon enquiring more and telling him tales that I had heard of journeys from Flores to Sumba using Pelni did he reply, "Oh, of course, we have ships that go to Sumba. I was assuming you were rather too keen on taking the ferry."

Two Pelni ships, Awu and Wilis, did the distance between Ende and Waingapu in Sumba as part of their long itinerary touching several islands. Everyone in Flores knew these names and talked about them as if they were popular film stars. But the mystery about them continued as we wanted to know more. Everyone outside of Ende had different views on the day they left Ende for Sumba. Some were certain that they left every alternate Monday; some said every Wednesday for Wilis and every Saturday for Awu; while some said that Wilis was old and retired.

When we came to Ende, there were obvious signs that these two mythical creatures were nearer. The uncertainty now was more about the time of the day it left for everyone claimed that the Wilis left every alternate Thursday morning while Awu left every alternate Monday. But while some said it left at night, others swore that it left during the day.

To set things straight, we headed for the Pelni office where the ojek drivers joined us to help decipher the codes. There was a very reassuring posted notice outside the Pelni office on the schedule of the ships. We chose Wilis which met our travel plans. It was a perfect arrangement of the universe; Wilis would leave Ende at a very convenient nine in the morning; so we could wake up late, have a glorious Indonesian breakfast of two small biscuits and coffee before boarding the ship, and we would be in Sumba by early evening. The ojek drivers advised us to take Ayu because it was a larger ship and would have a cinema inside but that didn't seem a good enough incentive to postpone our trip by four days.

Buying the tickets at Pelni was a breeze. The office had high walls and ancient teakwood furniture as all offices should have. The serious-looking official asked us to write down our details on a chit of paper and wait. The benches were occupied by people with faces representing the whole of Indonesia. There were ladies from Aceh wearing headscarves, Makassar people with their dark sun-burnt skins, a Javanese, and also a poor-looking Caucasian who had made Timor his home. A scrawny man sweeping the office floor ran to us as soon as he saw us and began making exaggerated gestures. He couldn't talk and we were wondering whether he was scolding us for having stepped on his cleaned job. But he kept pointing to his mouth and then to somewhere outside the gates. I thought he was asking us to explore the small *warungs* or small eateries so I said that I would go later. But his movements got more excited and only when I handed him a thousand rupiah, he ran away as swiftly as he had come.

"Alas, my people," we heard a voice. The young man who had blurted it out offered his hand to us. He was Ari Masu, a young software engineer from Timor. He looked how any software engineer should look, balding head, small physique, and a bit overweight from hours spent facing a box. He had come alone to Ende on a holiday and had avoided the popular Kelimutu even though he had never been there. He was a thinker, a philosopher, with a penchant for extrapolating everything from micro to macro. He said that he was also an activist who wrote on his blog about the problems afflicting Indonesia, particularly its governing classes. So it was obvious why he had avoided Kelimutu. He had spent his days in Ende under the replacement breadfruit tree of Sukarno and contemplated how his beloved country had moved away from the principles of Pancasila. When he heard that we were about to get married, he gave us a knowing smile, "Isn't it wonderful how rivers merge, cultures converge and different races find love in one another, and I am so honoured to have encountered you in this beautiful journey." We left him for a moment with his musings when our name was called.

The tickets cost us only about six dollars each and it looked like those beautiful air-tickets of golden days with multiple leaflets, a souvenir to share with many people along the way.

We were about to say goodbye to Ari Masu when he asked us what time our ferry was. "Never take the printed time for granted; never take anything for granted in my country. We took democracy and freedom for granted and then Suharto came." We told him that the Pelni officer had asked us to check the timing again on the day of travel because the seas were choppy and there could be delays. "Choppy seas, their favourite excuse, always choppy seas," Ari Masu continued in his hushed voice, "This is my country; we always blame the worst on everyone but ourselves." I was tempted to ask him what he thought about the erstwhile Indonesian occupation of Timor Leste but didn't dare to because that might have driven him into a frenzy. We hurriedly left the Pelni office nodding to everything Ari Masu had to stay. That whole day we avoided going anywhere near the Pancasila tree lest we got caught by Ari Masu again.

During the day, many of the people we came across spoke about the uncertainty with the ship's arrival, just as Ari Masu had warned, but with less drama. So we went back to the Pelni office that evening and indeed there was a notice that said that the ship will come fourteen hours later and then depart after an hour's stop at Ende. So far so good, because it gave us one extra day in Ende which we eventually used to go back to Pasar Ikan. But the next morning, Ari Masu sent a message, "Please check your ferry timing again, mine left four hours later than the time they put on the notice board, after already being late for ten hours," he went on to send more, "It's always like this here, the whole system is one big rot, there is no accountability." When we went to check the noticeboard again, the delay had increased by another six hours. So the ferry would now arrive at two past midnight and then leave at three. We were wondering why, after being already delayed for so long, did it not leave at a more convenient time the next day? But the very competent officer at Pelni that day told us that Pelni was highly committed to its schedule and it would go to great lengths to make sure that the delay was made up. It was an eight-hour journey from Ende to Waingapu in Sumba and he said that the latest news is that the winds are favourable and the seas are smiling gently, so it was definite that the journey could be made in only six hours.

To be fair to Pelni, this obsession with pretending to catch up with schedule was necessary because their ships usually travelled to many islands along their route, often almost covering the whole archipelago. Such journeys would take several weeks and if they tended to accept any slack not because of technical or weather related reasons, each journey could easily explode into months. For Wilis, the ship that we were taking, it travelled at a stretch for two weeks, starting from Makassar in Sulawesi Island, to Bima in Sumbawa, then Labuan Bajo in Flores, to Waingapu in Sumba, back to Flores to Ende, to Kupang in Timor, back to Ende, then to Waingapu again, then to Labuan Bajo, then Bima, Makassar, to Marapokot and Maumere in Flores again, then Larantuka in Flores, then Kupang, back to Larantuka, then Maumere, Marapokot; finally resting at Makassar, before taking off again along this route the next day. Wilis was a rat that frenetically visited the same place again and again, not in any particular order, but got forced into slowness by the choppy seas. All the other rats on Pelni's books followed similar circuits. One of them was proposed to be named Tongkat Ali, after the legendary traditional Indonesian Viagra. But Pelni dropped the name for some reason. I was sure that Ari Masu would have blamed it on choppy seas.

We had not been completely faithful to Wilis. We did go looking for a ferry to explore if we could reach Sumba earlier. Ende has two jetties, one for the ferries and one for Pelni. The one for ferries, located at a small bay called Ipi, had little more than one abandoned office building and a signboard that had been weathered by the elements. The bay was scenic but rough and when we were there, two old men were squatting by the barbed wire gate. They told us that the ferries left as and when they pleased and so we could leave our contacts with them and they will pass on to the right person. That man would call us whenever there were enough passengers. It sounded like a bemo, swimming around the coast of Ende in a zig-zag looking for bums, and we decided to remain loyal to Wilis.

Wilis was encroaching on our lives steadily even before we caught a sight of it. All we could think about was Wilis. How will we reach the ferry terminal so late at night? What if Wilis doesn't come on time? Will we be left stranded on a lonely concrete beach? Will Wilis only have wooden chairs to squeeze ourselves in? Will Wilis give us seasickness? How will the people on board at Wilis treat us? Is it possible that Wilis may sink? Did Ari Masu ever meet Wilis?

The hotel owner again disputed Pelni's claim to arrive at two past midnight and said that it will surely reach Ende by midnight. A few of the roaming ojek drivers confidently told us that it would be reaching around four in the morning. Everyone in Ende waits for Wilis at different times.

After much asking around, we arranged for Pak Banggo's nephew and his friend to drop us to the ferry terminal on their motorbikes. It was a perfect arrangement in a newly familiar city. They were familiar characters and since they didn't drive ojeks for a living, they were charging us much less. Other ojek drivers were asking us a price that was as much as the entire Pelni trip from Ende to Sumba. But these two were also young men, university students. So there was little chance that they would have woken up at two in the night. And so it turned out. We called them and messaged them several times but all we could hear was the buzz of the careless snoring of mobile phones.

Half awake, we stood outside our hotel, hoping to get someone to take us to the jetty. I couldn't think properly. I was dreaming that gods of all religions from human history were organizing a conference with all the characters of all novels written yet, to discuss how to solve an ancient sewage problem. The whole town slept. Everything was pitch black. Not even a dog was passing by. I could hear Lobo's clock ticking like a hammer in my head. Everything was still. There was no way of going to anywhere.

After waiting for twenty minutes, we found a man in a motorcycle approaching. We were no longer in a state of mind to respond to anything and just watched him pass by. For some reason, he stopped and came back to us. He was not an ojek driver but we explained to him our situation. He looked at Lobo and asked me, "Where is she from, China or Japan?" Not a good sign. Why does he need to know where Lobo comes from? He proposed to take me first to the jetty, then come back to the hotel and take Lobo. Why is he so keen to help us? But in our minds, yet to be fully alert from waking up at this unusual hour, we agreed to the suggestion. I asked Lobo not to get on his bike till I called her.

The man was probably in his forties, dark complexioned, with wavy hair. He kept on talking as we reached the jetty in five minutes. The army personnel guarding the entrance told us that the ship will come in an hour. I asked the motorcycle driver to wait until I called Lobo but as happens in the best of times; my phone couldn't catch any signal. He couldn't understand why he must wait and without giving me much time to react, got on his bike and left. My muddled mind was clearing up in panic and it began pondering about the various casualties that could happen to Lobo. What if the man took Lobo somewhere in this sleeping city? What if he just took all her money? How will I find Lobo?

I kept trying to call her. Sweat appeared on my brows. But within ten minutes, the man came back with Lobo. I wanted to hug him. I wanted to hug Lobo. I wanted to scream, "Humanity is alive and well." We paid him a token amount for his help which he smilingly accepted.

Only after I had Lobo beside me, I became conscious of what was around me. Many people had assembled at the waiting area, which was a spacious but dimly-lit hall with blue wooden benches along its edges. The air was numb; everyone was staring into some blankness. Some of them had come from villages around Ende and had been waiting for more than a day outside the premises. They had big bags made of Technicolor plastic sheets. Some men were still smoking, lazily raising the hand with the cigarette to their lips and then dropping it lifeless. Babies slept like bows without strings on their mother's laps. The only active people were the ones wearing helmets. They were moving around jovially. They were the ojek drivers waiting for passengers. Someone spotted the lights of Wilis. Half the waiting room got up and headed for the jetty like a bunch of mother turtles limping to the seas after a tiring night of once-a-year egg laying. I couldn't see anything but we all kept looking at the faint border between the sea and the night sky.

Then it was there. First a torch light, then a small incandescent bulb, then a big car lamp, and finally a ship, lit like an electric angel wearing a veil of hanging candles. It honked announcing its arrival and all of us stood at the edge of the long jetty, hoping to have a good look at the lovely bride. It was possible that some of us may have just jumped and swam gently to the ship; so long had we all waited. The army came with their megaphones, asking us turtles to step back. We stepped back, just that little bit. One man standing next to us assumed responsibility for us. He was perhaps in his sixties with a big moustache, cap and a much used denim jacket very typical of Indonesians. He asked us to beware of pickpockets. He offered us some cake and water and asked us to follow him once the ship arrived. It was 4 in the morning.

The ship seemed to be stationary, just happy to show off its glitter. But it did come closer and closer. The full moon kept falling as gentle waves ran slowly to the shore and then went back. The crowd assembled again and this time the army created a fjord in between so that the people alighting could pass. A mass of smooth rounded helmets, all reflecting the moon, stood at the front, most anxious to greet people, familiar and new. The ojek drivers were closing in for the hunt. We too kept moving forward, in small steps. Did some of us fall off? But everything was quiet, very quiet. The Machiavellian resource-grabber in me was getting anxious. Were we too far behind? How will it be inside? Will we end up with the worst seats?

Wilis docked and blew its horn twice. Suddenly there was an unfamiliar rush. The army stepped in and things came to a standstill again. Wilis was big, almost like a cruise ship. A man ran through the fjord that the army had created, holding a listless young girl in his arms. She had fainted. We didn't know if she was one of those alighting or one of us who finally gave in to the anxiety of anticipation. A small stream of the alighting passengers went through, avoiding our gazes. It was nineteen hours past Wilis' scheduled time of departure.

We got pulled in. For the first time in Indonesia, I was surrounded by a sense of urgency among the people. They were surely bulldozing for the best seats. We lost contact with our godfather. Holding Lobo's hands, I followed one person's back to another person's back. A river was flowing up over its delta. I was just following the commands of all the pushing and shuffling behind me. It was hard to see. It was hard to breathe. I hit the staircase of Wilis. Once on it, the order of the universe couldn't be changed anymore. Each one of us finally had his place in the world.

The first sights were not too appetising. A bunch of men stood on the railings, topless. Beside the entrance gates, some women were sleeping on the floor. We entered and inside it was a world of metal in grease-stained white. Signboards in French words told us the way to our assigned seats; but did it matter in this rumble? The lights were yellow and greasy too. The air was heavy with cigarettes. The sleeping chambers had beds in two rows facing each other, a number on top of each. All right, so we won't have to squat on the floor. The passengers were all sitting, looking at us with dead eyes. Why were they awake at this hour? Some were especially cautious. They had spread out their luggage on top of their bed; squeezing in somehow in the remaining space and keeping a watchful eye for the flies. The mattresses had been stripped off from some of the beds. Later we found them with the women who were sleeping outside. This was their way to escape the cigarette smog. The crowd got thinner and thinner as we walked along. Then at one corner, we found two beds along the wall, waiting for us.

No one had taken our seats as were indicated in our tickets. Why was there such a rush to get on board then? Perhaps it was caused by those who wanted to rip off the mattresses for an alfresco trip.

We settled in and let our backpacks rest on the floor. Will they be stolen? I couldn't yet relax in my new home. There were ten other passengers in our section. Their eyeballs settled on us. We just quietly smiled at each other and they went back into their state of horizontal slumber except for one woman who kept sitting and looking at us.

A starved looking cockroach was moving over my assigned bed. I knew I wouldn't be able to sleep for I was the original inspiration for Andersen's children's tale, "The princess and the pea". I can eat any cooked worm in the world, or travel on vans running on square wheels, or for that matter stay passive in front of the greatest injustices in the world. But displace me from the bed, bolster, pillow and the bedroom I am used to, and the chances are high that, overnight, I would be able to finish counting the wool on the sheep. One of the men in the rows of beds facing us began to play music on his phone so that everyone in his group could hear. I lay on my stomach and faced the wall. Many things were written in those grimy walls, the usual American movie slangs and abuses.

I began to develop a headache from the smoke. I looked up and saw innocent looking smoke detectors on the walls that had lost their voice. I changed sides many times. By then Lobo was fast asleep. Perhaps she was only pretending. The lady who was sitting and staring at us earlier was still sitting and staring at the number on top of my bed. The giant toilet doors, all thick metal, kept banging in a rhythm. I imagined barnacles rising up from the bottom of Wilis and chewing my fingers. I got up and walked around like the brightest minds and angel headed hipsters of the beat poet Allen Ginsberg's generation.

The whole ship looked like a bomb shelter from inside. The doors were big and heavy. Styrofoam takeaway packs and burnt cigarette butts formed unknown fractals on the floor, especially under the beds. Women stretched inside toilets marked for men and men assembled for a smoke outside the women's. A man was walking around with a basket hanging from his neck. He was offering rice with fried chicken in packets that everyone was buying eagerly. At this hour? Fried chickens at this hour? A young man came running out of one of the bathrooms, wearing only a towel. I was losing sense of time. I went inside one of the metal chambers, the only men's toilet I could find with no women inside. It was flooded with water that looked clean but suspicious. I went back to my bed and began falling inside an endless whirlpool.

I pretended to wake up a few hours later. Lobo was awake and sitting, staring at the woman who was still sitting and staring. Her husband was sitting next to her, slowly eating fried chicken from the styrofoam pack. They were coming from Kupang and were on their way to Bima. The other passengers were a group of people from Makassar who worked in Kupang and were going home. This bunch of people would be travelling for three days on Wilis and seemed well prepared for it. Each one took turns to play songs on their mobile phones so that there would be a continuous stream of music. They also seemed to have an endless flow of jokes. At one time, they began taking photos of one another, posing like cowboys and American rowdy rappers and Baywatch super-heroes. Then they began ganging up on the leader of the group by forcing him to take off his shirt, put on huge dark glasses, and hold an empty plastic bottle like a sceptre. They rolled all over the dirty floor trying to recover from uncontrollable laughter and pleaded us to take pictures of their compromised superhero.

After our laughter subsided, we went around having a look again. Most of the passengers were awake, some playing cards, some watching movies on their laptops, some just staring over bed tops. While it was the same grimy yellow inside, outside, the sun was bright and the sky a cloudless blue. But we had come out at the wrong side of Pelni and it felt like all the bathroom liquids were being dumped into the sea from that deck. Even amidst this strong stench of urine, lovers stood together looking out at the beautiful blue while the strong breeze swept their hair into handsome manes. Eagerly, they made space for us and we struck the same pose as they all had, worthy of any low budget movie poster. But the breeze kept bringing the smell of urine to us with gusto and we decided to leave. Surprisingly the deck on the other side had no such smell. But this side faced the sun and so there were fewer people. But it was a delightful place with no trace of cigarette smoke. I felt like calling the lovers from the other deck to come over here.

The three railings on the deck neatly divided the sea into heaven, hell and somewhere in between. The breeze made us forget the sun. Suddenly it dawned on me that we had hardly made any arrangements for our wedding. There was indeed the pssoibility that after this trip, we would realize that we were not compatible with one another. But I found all the more reasons to want to be with Lobo for the rest of my life. More than halfway through our trip, we had already gone through tough travel experiences only to smile later holding each other's hands. The splendid moments at Kelimutu and onboard our boat in Komodo

Bay had foretold the possibility of more magic moments that we could enjoy together. Increasingly, I was feeling connected to her and to all the people we met, and the nature around us. To the people of Indonesia, we were already introducing ourselves as *Swami-Isteri* or husband and wife and not as *pacar* or girlfriend-boyfriend. Suddenly, I spotted a flying fish. It was a streak of sliver flashing over the blue and then disappearing as a glitter. I showed it to Lobo but she couldn't find it. Both of us are on opposite ends of the spectrum when it comes to spotting things. I am an exaggerated spotter who, if posted at NASA, would have found life in all the asteroids. Lobo would have missed it on earth. But she believed me for once and kept looking and soon there was a flurry of glitter. The flying fish came in tens and then hundreds, jumping in long leaps and great speed, teaching the birds how to swim.

Perhaps I wouldn't have minded staying all my life stuck at this moment, in this centre of the universe, only if the women moved away from the men's toilets.

When we got bored of eternity and went back inside, the Makassar boys were carrying mountains of food packets. "We eat two packets each," the leader of the gang grinned. It was their time for a holiday. Their happiness had already begun. They were going home.

The ship also had first class cabins that came with two beds with white sheets and red blankets. There was even a bolster. The cabins came with a study table and a personal toilet though we didn't go in to see if the floor there was also filled with water. There were thin red carpets on the floor and a small round window looking out into the sea. These went for thirty dollars. Loneliness came with a price. The first class people could eat at a separate restaurant with garish table cloth and cloth napkins.

We came down to the common pantry. It gave food only at scheduled times and we had missed that slot. The Makassar boys offered us to join them before they dug in but we pretended to be vain. We reached the snack bar which was still open. The bar had a sitting area with wooden benches; just like my earlier idea of Pelni. And these benches were packed with people who were sitting there to watch a film that was being played on TV. The two men at the counter advised us to go to the kitchen and ask the cooks for proper food because over there, they sold only peanuts and bottled tea, the national drink of Indonesia known as *teh botol*. "Ask the cooks there nicely," they advised us because it was after scheduled hours.

At this snack bar, I noticed the eighth modern wonder of the world, right in front of me, inside the refrigerator with the glass door, with the Coca Cola labels on the sides. It was a giant clock and a clock that showed the time accurately. They used the refrigerator to keep the clock and it was the first working clock we had seen since we had come to Flores. We almost jumped with excitement. In every hotel we had stayed at, in every restaurant we had patronised, and every house we had visited, we had never seen a clock in Flores that gave the correct time. They were always working, moving their needles arrogantly, in a time zone far away from their own. In fact, in one of the street markets at Ruteng, I had even seen an alarm clock that moved counter clockwise; a clock that was the antithesis of itself, something none of those high sounding Swiss companies had yet being able to make. The storeowner had still bothered to display it, hoping that some customer would mentally calculate the actual time every time he looked at it. But this one, inside the fridge, was perfect. Perhaps it was the cool temperature, it worked, and we kept looking at this technological wonder for longer than anyone had ever looked at a clock.

The kitchen was a huge storeroom of chimes, steel utensils hanging from all points in space, anxious to strike a cacophony. There was steel everywhere, giant steel vats, steel washing basins, steel trolleys and steel pipes criss-crossing the whole room. Two young cooks were still working. They were frying a thousand fish in a swimming pool of boiling oil. Behind them, was a small hill of deep fried chicken legs. The heads of the fish kept bobbing in the oil with lifeless eyes, just like kois do in a crowded pond in response to a few bread crumbs. The cooks were looking rather fashionable with their bespoke kitchen napkins and bandanas. The kitchen was closed for now and they were preparing for dinner. "Every day, we cook for over two thousand people three times," said one of them. Their bodies and faces were well toned and their spirits were high. They spoke with exaggerated hand gestures. "We will do something special for you even though the kitchen is officially closed," one of the men wrote down what he can offer in a small piece of paper, his small pencil stuck above his ears. "It would be fried drumsticks, some boiled spinach and white rice." After he wrote it down like a French waiter, he pasted the paper on his sweaty forehead with a slap and asked us to wait at the captain's cabin next door.

The captain's cabin had a bird, as any sea captain should have. The cage was too big for the bird and it flew around like an angry diva wanting to show us its moods. The captain's cage was small and after accommodating a dining place and a study table with a large ancient computer, one had to turn sideways to move around. The captain was in his forties and energetic despite being in the sea continuously for four months. After the initial introductions, he kept on asking us, "Why didn't you take the first class cabins? It is cheap. It's so much nicer. I can't understand why?" He counted all the reasons we should have gone for those cages. I asked if they had a bird in each. He chose to stay focused on why we should always travel on those cabins going forward.

One of the cooks came in to deliver the food. The label on his forehead distracted the captain from his cherished topic. We were much relieved. The food was largely in line with expectations from our Indonesia trip so far. But its saving grace was that it was hot. The aroma quietened the bird and put it to sleep.

On the wall of the captain's cabin, there was a big map of the archipelago. It had been printed in old times when Timor Leste was still part of Indonesia and West Papua was known as Irian Jaya Barat. Like all maps, this map had a force of gravity that attracted us and after finishing food, we got pulled towards it. That is the power of maps; they always draw people to them, young and old. They make us stand near them, mumble faintly the printed names, put fingers on dots, boast where all we have been, and plan where all we should go next. Maps are such a great way to kill time that we spent a good fifteen minutes doing exactly those things. Till a few decades back, the maps made one kill time by inciting wars. Perhaps colonialism and imperialism were as much a result of maps as maps were a result of them. Nowadays, they draw less attention but still provide a good few minutes of day dreaming.

We came back to the grimy dim light of our economy class section. There was an air of permanence and infinity in the cabin. The heavy metal doors of the toilets kept banging against the walls, dividing time like the cuckoos did for Garcia Lorca. All these doors had outgrown the space in the wall for them and were no longer lockable. From the small round window next to my bed, the sea ran by tirelessly.

But we were still far from Sumba. An announcement, "We have been delayed by four hours because of choppy seas." A bunch of men dressed in white made the rounds to check our tickets. They asked the men to stop smoking and pretended to be surprised why the smoke detectors were not working.

Soon after, men and women with baskets made rounds, trying to sell another round of packet food. The cleaners, the real heroes of these ships, came every two hours. They were the mythical gods, attempting to achieve the impossible. Just their sheer intent was laudable. The big plastic trash bags, one in each section, got filled up with white Styrofoam packs in no time. Cigarette stubs spread over the floor like wildfire and the toilets got flooded faster than a tsunami. Bugs made love and burped out babies at the speed of nuclear reactions. But these cleaners still came, quietly moved around like industrial robots and without complaining to anyone, disappeared. Their work didn't seem to make much difference to the filth around. But one needs to ponder what might have happened if they were not around. Pillars of Styrofoam packs, more impressive than any Roman columns, would have supported the roofs. The ship might have even sunk from the weight of bugs.

I tried to sleep again. It was impossible. I pretended. I could hear my heartbeat. Time had stuck in rust. I thought I was in the middle of a sun-baked field. I couldn't see anything for miles. A man came with his scarecrow and began changing its clothes. He made it put on one shirt after another. The scarecrow kept grinning. It was his birthday. I got up, looked around. A wave of people was swaying gently. I huddled in my bed, avoiding their gaze. Nothing was moving, nothing was changing. I ran for the doors.

Outside, there was land in the shape of a pyramid whose top had been shaved off neatly. It looked like the Komodo and Rinca islands, arid, coated with bushy grass. This was Sumba. It stayed like that for another two hours, never coming closer, as if the ship was swimming on a treadmill.

In an eternity, the time finally came, the ship honked like a baritone elephant. Before we realized anything, the people sharing our cabin got up and came to wish us an enjoyable stay. We had arrived four hours later than planned.

As we walked leisurely up to the exit, there was a crowd with giant bags on each shoulder. We were the last in the queue to get out and we stayed at the foot of the stairs inside the cabin for another fifteen minutes before there was any movement. And then the hustle followed, people moving in small steps, getting closer and closer to each other. Soon they were embracing the bags on the back of the person in front of them. Bags squeezed us from the sides as well. Pelni officials held a rope at the sides to maintain order. One man's job was just to look for burning cigarettes and he pulled them out of the mouths of passengers. "It is dangerous," he explained diligently to each one of them from whom he pulled out the cigarettes. These hapless people could barely protest as their hands were rendered immobile by the bags on all sides.

The pressure eased as soon as we got out of the ship entrance. We were back among ojeks and bemos. We saw the caterpillar waiting for us. We walked towards it like freed animals. Looking back, KM Wilis was fine and majestic in white. It was warm, sunny and clear. It was Waingapu. It was Sumba.

One night stand with civilization

Waingapu is the largest town in Sumba and its administrative capital. It lies at the edge of East Sumba and for most foreigners, it is merely a transit town on their way to the famed traditional villages of West Sumba where Christianity and Islam still struggle to completely win over traditionally conditioned minds. All the same, we made a sudden decision to stay over at Waingapu for the night to recover from the passive smoking on-board Wilis. Hurriedly, we looked for a hotel in our guidebook and two ojeks to take us there.

We were dazzled by the colours on display at Waingapu as we had got used to the monotonous dark green of wet Flores. Huge bougainvillea bushes formed colourful arches along the road. Lime green was back in fashion among the foliage. Pastel colored houses sat pretty in large courtyards. But the heat soon overtook our delight and we realized that Waingapu was not a city of the day. The streets were barren, even at the town centre. A few faces could be seen hiding behind the windows. The ojeks dropped us and ran away to the nearest shade.

When we looked carefully, there was a lot of life beneath each shade. Mobile *warungs* selling bakso and other trinkets had assembled under the big trees. They called out to us instead of bringing over their carts. Fresh from the dim of Wilis, we were yet to be wary of the sun. As we reached them, one man took out a giant papaya out of his trousers' pocket and offered it to us! That was the only thing he had to sell. We asked if he could cut it for us and that put him into some disarray. He asked around for a knife and we could see his desperation rising as he didn't manage to find one. Finally, one shoe repairer gave him a sharp blade. It was only good for cutting leather and the man struggled to make pieces. But he persisted and won against the papaya.

We took up a place in Hotel Elvin, the most sophisticated hotel in our entire trip. We were hypnotised by the opulence. No more pink bum-shaped buckets to move around hot water. We had in Elvin, two taps pointing boldly towards two directions, hot and cold. There was an air conditioner and a hair dryer. For the first time, we had white bed sheets and crisp brown blankets. There was even a neat balcony from where we could sit like an old couple and watch the construction for the renovation of the hotel's inner wing. We spent the afternoon contemplating the papaya and slowly consuming it in the mood for Zen.

As the sun went down, we ventured out to see what Waingapu had to offer and it had turned up as the vain Casanova. Stalls with giant incandescent bulbs lined the streets. Men moved around holding big bunch of Technicolor balloons. At street corners, merry-go-rounds and toy trains had suddenly sprung up doing their eternal rounds. People filled the streets; overweight women walking with their puffy cheeked children; lean young men pacing frenetically in all directions, blaring ojeks and pedal rickshaws densely decorated with small blinking bulbs imitating the Milky Way. Many of these rickshaws came with sound systems; different party themes passed by us, some trance, some hip-hop and some just music in midi format. Old women selling steamed peanuts sat on the kerbs maintaining equal distances between them like milestones. In between them, there were makeshift eateries on carts, selling satay, or various deep fried snacks, known in Indonesia as '*Aneka Gorengan*'. Behind them were large curtains with primary school pictures of chicken, duck, and different kinds of catfish. These curtains, used all over Indonesia by *warungs* selling grilled fish and chicken, serve as both advertisement banners and cover for customers. They would have the same combination of words everywhere, *Pecel Lele, Ayam Goreng, Bebek Bakar* and *Tempe Penyet*. The paintings on these curtains were uniform across Indonesia suggesting that they were mass manufactured; perhaps by some Indonesian Titian.

All these disappeared by eight in the night. Every day, Waingapu woke up from its slumber for only two hours, between six and eight, dazzled in its lights, balloons and smells, and then followed the advice of the elderly to sleep early.

We headed for the main Pasar or market of Waingapu. It was the kingdom of *sirih pinang,* the name used to denote the combination of betel nuts, dry or unripe, and bundled sticks of asparagus-like stalks or *sirih* of the betel. Every other shop had heaps of these piled up as if Christmas was approaching. We walked around aimlessly and people called us from every direction to have a small chat. This place had not seen many visitors after all. Mothers woke up their babies to show how foreigners looked like. "Take a picture of my kids," cried one mother.

We passed by the fish section of the market on to the chicken section, where we met John Kumis or John Moustache, who asked us to call him Chicken Uncle. Chicken Uncle and his friends were winding down their business for the day, "It has been a good day for business." That showed in the chicken's eyes which had seen enough slaughters for the day. "Take pictures of our best chicken, this one; here, this one. He has a nice one too." Some indeed had plumage worthy of any Native American king. We gave them a bag of *sirih pinang* and they taught us how to consume it. "It is easier than learning how to swim; chew the betel nut, bite off some of the sirih stalk and keep chewing, take in some lime powder; wait for the mouth to feel like it's full of water, then spit out only the water when you can't hold it anymore." He forgot to add that you can also observe the blood-red spit that you have just let out, then expose your stained teeth to people around you. "Keep chewing." All this while, it is customary to laugh without any reason. "Pick one more betel nut and stalk and repeat the same process. Continue for the rest of the day." Then take a break only for having your meals and for sleep. "Continue once you wake up the next day."

Chicken Uncle and other people whom we met later in Sumba explained that this chewing of *sirih pinang* has significant cultural importance. The betel nut represents the female reproductive spirit while the sirih obviously represents the male. The white lime powder is supposed to represent the virile sperm. "The red spit is the symbol of bloody childbirth," Said Chicken Uncle. *Sirih pinang* dominates all social exchanges in South East Asia but has slowly been eroding from customs and memories. But it still remains of utmost importance in Sumba. Every one we came across had pouches well stocked with *sirih pinang*. With so many of the shops selling *sirih pinang* in such huge quantities, replenishing the stock was never an issue. The pouches were offered when one met strangers or went to a new village as a symbol of friendliness. "If you refuse these offerings, it is very very bad," said Chicken Un cle; this could imply extreme rudeness to the point of an invitation to open hostility, one to be settled with spilling of actual blood. "If you take it and then throw it away in front of me, that means you want to fight with my whole community now." One also offers *sirih pinang* when visiting someone's house, asking for a woman's hand for marriage or just to visit a village as a tourist.

The chewing of *sirih pinang* is considered a sign of maturity, something adults do to chill, something cool. It is also a way to have fun with the few tourists who come to Sumba. Let them chew, act like a chicken in front of screeching car brakes, and have a good laugh at them. It is mildly addictive and can bring a hint of intoxication for the uninitiated. That explains the obsession with chewing non-stop. Otherwise, there can be little reason to continuously re-enact on a mass scale this distantly symbolic unification of male and female gametes to produce babies.

We promised to send Chicken Uncle pictures of his chickens and himself with his friends. But his address sounded rather unreachable: Chicken Uncle at Pasar Ayam or Chicken Market in Waingapu, Sumba. We checked with him a few times and he swore by it. Our suspicions were true as when we sent him the pictures after we came back to Singapore, he never received them. But this was his only address he knew; he slept on top of the chicken coop.

We took Chicken Uncle's advice and went to a restaurant called Mr Café, the highlight of Waingapu food culture. On the way we passed by some of the informal chains of Indonesia, stalls selling *Bakso Solo* and shops with names like Salon Surabaya and Pangkas Rambut Surabaya. Somehow, all over Indonesia, one comes across these shops and stalls. They are not under any single brand and just use the association of the name with the cities in Indonesia, Solo and Surabaya in these cases, to get loyal customers. So all *bakso* stalls that sell noodles with an egg, meat broth and beef balls, claim to follow the style of Solo. And a considerable number of hair cutting salons claim to be run by people coming from Surabaya because they do it the best. The grapevine has it that all these Surabaya migrants working at hair salons are transvestites or gays who also offer other services. We peeped into a few and found reasonable reasons to suspect the same.

Lobo was delighted with Mr Café not only because we had more choices than just ordering the bland Southern Chinese stuff but also because there were enough cats to give us company. By now, the cats and dogs in Flores had passed on the news to Sumba that we were a group of tourists who loved to share our food with four-legged animals, even though rather miserly. The petite and humble manager of Mr Café; incidentally there were no Mr or male at that place, came every five minutes to grab the cats by the waist, slap their heads lovingly, and plead with them to not bother us. But the cats grumbled and kept coming to us.

When we came out of Mr Café, the city was dozing off. The glittering rickshaws were gone and the playful toy trains had been put to sleep with grey plastic sheet blankets. The only lights along the road were coming from the sachet selling shops. Indonesia is a sachet country where more than a third of fast moving consumer products are sold as sachets. Here, almost everything can be found in sachets. There are sachets for the usual suspects: shampoo, conditioner, coffee and tea mixes. But there are also sachets for popsicles, jellies, tobacco, biscuits, peanuts, chilli paste, and even car wash. They are everywhere, inside every glass showcase, on top of all counters, hanging like vines over any available support. Indonsian saying: "One can never extract the last drop out of a sachet."

The next day, despite the white bedsheets, breakfast at Hotel Elvin was the familiar combination of one sweet bread and one cup of tea. This too was the leitmotif for our Indonesia trip. For every breakfast, we were invariably offered the same combination. But before one gets the impression that there is one great chain like Pizza Hut running a standardized breakfast delivery chain in Indonesia, one has to note that there are subtle yet life-changing differences. For instance, sometimes it is coffee and sometimes its tea. And every bread has a unique soul, sometimes its peanut, sometimes sugar and butter, sometimes a dark abyss. Some really kind-hearted hotels threw in a small banana with this; the one in Bajawa split a passion fruit into halves. Invariably they would mention a breakfast in their sales pitch to us when we went bargain hunting for rooms. And some hotels would have elaborate spaces with over twenty tables just for this breakfast offering as they rarely served lunches or dinners. But at the time of breakfast, we would see at most one of these tables occupied, with just one person sitting there, slowly contemplating global warming next to the small plate kept at the edge of the great table. But with this simple offering, Losmen Agung at Ruteng had won our heart. Because when I had asked them about breakfast, theirs was the only one that denied serving breakfast and still diligently served the coffee-bread combo. And even more, they would serve it to the rooms and make rounds to see if we needed a refill. No wonder, Losmen Agung is the best hotel even if it is the most rickety hotel. As Mandarin Oriental would have put it, two of us were fans.

We left the hotel early in the morning for one final walk around the streets of Waingapu because by now Lobo had come to love the place for its colors and simplicity. The handicrafts vendors greeted us. These vendors are rather unique in Waingapu. They assemble around the hotels in small numbers and stay outside the gates all day and night whenever they hear from their grapevine that some tourists had arrived. There, they spread out their small collection, a few small bronze and wooden statues, cases to keep the lime for *sirih pinang*, ikat weavings, and a few beads. Whenever a hotel guest enters or exits the hotel gates, these vendors smile at them and ask them to have a look. They have an air of numbness about them, perhaps from waiting at the same place all day. Like zombies, they don't talk, just raise a hand to point to their collection and grin. Any American management expert would have exclaimed that there is an agency problem there; these vendors are not shareholders themselves. But they are. Just that they haven't read American books on management. It almost seemed like either they were aliens or we were. We couldn't talk to each other. They could only point to things, grin and quote a price. Occasionally they will spread out their wings to expose the full ikat length. But when we were about to leave the hotel and board the bemo for Waikabubak, the wind from our movements stuck a lightning at the zombies and they came to life. They hurried behind us, holding statues and ikat. They had found language, bringing down prices by big amounts every second like a radioactive decay. A little bronze rhinoceros that I had gazed at for slightly longer fell from eighty dollars to five. The rhinoceros had a sullen look. They stood in front of the bemo's windows, pleading. The windows were closed and we could only offer them fake tourist smiles and good byes in return.

Finally, the land of roofs and skies

Waikabubak lives in a world of its own. Concrete encroaches around bamboo. Tall pointed tin roofs climb over tall pointed thatch roofs. Traditional villages, that occupy the vantage points on top of small hills, look over the modern-day Indonesian shops and houses below, always ready to defend. Countless mud trails weave off from the narrow concrete roads forming deltas. Village heads on horses walk past senior government officials in netted vans.

We were finally at the heart of Sumba culture and the spirit of *Marapu*, the traditional religion of the Sumbanese, was around us. In West Sumba, around Waikabubak, men still fought each other on horseback every year as part of the ritual festival of Pasola. And only in and around Waikabubak, despite several attempts by the Indonesian government including imposition of a slaughter tax, burials still involve ceremonial killing of large animals and elaborate rituals of building, moving and filling megalithic tombs.

And what is *Marapu*? It seems like an implausibly complicated concept. None of the people we met in Sumba, whether guide, priest or *kepala kampung*, could explain to us clearly. It is perhaps best described as another world that lies in between the god, who being the almighty has no name and little time or need to deal with anything, and the living humans, a world infested with ancestral spirits and a lot more. Some call it a religion. But the Indonesian government refused to recognise it as a religion that can be filled in forms. Perhaps *Marapu* is more of a physical space infested with mysterious characters that influences life as we know. Or perhaps it is just a collection of rituals governing key events in life, birth, death, weddings, inheritance, or conflict resolution. It is both singular and a collective. It is a continuum but it is perhaps also an individual ancestor. It is both diverse within the community, with each village having its own peculiar set of rituals, while being homogenous in broad sense. Every clan has its own *Marapu* as do natural objects such as the birds, mountains and the sea. Some Sumbanese believe that the sun and the moon were a divine couple whose union gave birth to eight male and female spirits. These spirits began to descend the many layers of heaven above the earth and once on earth, separated and formed couples among themselves to give rise to human clans. In day-to-day life, the concept of *Marapu* is perhaps not very different from the practices of the tribes of Flores and Sumbawa, essentially meaning ritualised interpretations of everything around us and ritualised counter of these omens, often through animal sacrifices, mediated by the high priest called the *Rato*.

The journey from Waingapu to Waikakbubak didn't provide many hints. Our bemo circled around Waingapu for three hours looking for passengers and it took another four hours to cover the one hundred and twenty kilometres of road that separated the two towns. On top of our bemo were three dogs who were squealing during the whole journey. Their mouths had been tied with straw and to their necks was attached a thick bamboo fragment so that they wouldn't run off. Since they were surrounded with big baskets, we initially thought that they were part of a family that was moving residence. But later we were told that the Sumbanese, like many other Indonesians, love to eat dog meat, and these baby-squealing creatures were being transported for a feast. Dogs are much more expensive in West Sumba than in the east, so lots are transported this way and end up in the Waitabula market.

On the bemo, we also met Jimmy. Jimmy was the *konjak*, de-facto manager of the bemo. He would hang from its door for the entire seven hours of its journey and give out death-screams to warn the driver whenever the bemo was approaching another vehicle or corner, "Ojajajajajaja". He also howled whenever he saw a prospective passenger, "Oioioioioioi." Jimmy wasn't scared of accidents, it was just his style. He looked like Axl Rose, though only four feet tall, a man perhaps in his early twenties, with wavy hair and toned muscles. He lived on the edge as much as a man who was a helper in a bemo could. When we stopped midway for a break, Jimmy spent the entire ten minutes styling his hair. If he had been born in Singapore, he would have got an intricate name like Aloisius or Harville, names much in fashion there. At the least, he deserved a name like Adonis Kecil or mini-Adonis. Instead, he ended up as Jimmy. Nonetheless, Jimmy had assumed responsibility for us and made sure that we could get as much comfort as possible in that sardine packed bemo. He would keep asking passengers to move their bags a little and slide their bums a bit to give us that extra millimetre of premium bum-space.

But the driver of the bemo was the antithesis of Jimmy. With a ponytail and kind cow-like eyes, Daniel didn't seem to be hassled by anything. A young man was half-sitting on his lap all the way while he drove, but his head kept swinging to the music. He waved and screamed a joyful hello to all drivers coming from the opposite direction. Whenever Jimmy gave out a Munch scream, Daniel would give him a playful glance. In between these two, the passengers sat dead stiff. Perhaps conscious of our presence, they wanted to disappear into their seats as much as they could. One petite girl sat out all the seven hours like a Praying Mantis, carrying a bag as big as herself on her lap, not flinching once. This very remarkable Indonesian capacity to hibernate into a numb state was very practical in such situations. If there were great surfs within their minds, building up water behind the dam, it didn't show in their eyes.

Sumba is known as the Texas of Indonesia for its barren landscape with men on horses. From high vantages along the road, we saw miles upon miles of rolling hills covered with yellow-tinged green grass and shrubs. An occasional mirror lake appears, the rest is all grass, grass, grass, waiting to dry in the sun. Jimmy tells us, "In the height of summer, the grass is all burned away and you see only the earth." Only as one approaches Waikabubak, which is a good six hundred metres above sea level, the landscape changes, with stretches of eucalyptus and temperate tree forests.

Sumba is indeed a fabled land for horses, to eat as much as they want, then take a roll downhill, run amok with friends, jump over bushes chasing dragonflies, pause to make love, and brood under the stars.

Trading of horses had been one of the mainstays of the Sumbanese economy till the recent past. Even now, lots of them are exported on the ferry from Waikelo to Sape, Sumbawa to pull cidomos or small horse carts in Sumbawa and Lombok. As for humans, Sumba also had a thriving business of trading human slaves within and outside the island. Even now, Sumbanese society has a substantial proportion of people classified as slaves who enjoyed little privileges in society. They are called '*orang dalam rumah*' or 'people inside the house'.

Apart from the horses, Sumba is also the home of the white cows. These white cows dazzled in the bright sunlight of arid Sumba. Children of the sun on stilted legs; we had to take off our eyes lest we were blinded.

Once in Waikabubak, we set about our now well-practiced hobby of hotel hunting and settled for Hotel Artha. Artha is located off from the main streets of Waikabubak, in between residential quarters. As we walked towards Artha, locals greeted us enthusiastically. With our heavy backpacks turning us into Sherpa porters on a trek up Chomolungma, it was not the most opportune time for *obrol* or small talk and we had to excuse ourselves. The dogs took note of our rudeness and approached us like wolves. Lobo, who has patented a technique of dealing with such dogs, came to my rescue. While remaining a Sherpa, she pretended to pick up pebbles and the wolves turned back into petty dogs. I loved this psychological play and for the rest of my stay, looked forward to such interactions with dogs.

There is Waikabubak of the day and Waikabubak of the night. Then there is Waikabubak of the early morning. During the day, the town puts up pretence of vastness and importance. There are two main roads in Waikabubak, wide and dusty, forming a big T. One of these roads began with big grocery stores run by the Chinese, then got lined by the government buildings, occasional hotels, the town stadium, the churches, a huge police station and ended at the town's borders with the two so-called best restaurants of Waikabubak, again run by the Chinese. The other road began midway along the previous road and at right-angles to it, passed by various shops, led to the main market or Pasar, got bordered by two big crafts and antique stores managed by people of Arab descent, before ending in unimportance. The T junction of these two roads was marked by a leaning light post, the leaning tower of Waikabubak, with Technicolor smaller lights hanging from it.

The main Pasar was more a reservoir of rot and smell of waste. Only in Waikabubak, salt was sold as ice-creams, heaped into that familiar shape on cones. During nights, the town remained awake only along this road, that too till eight after which the leaning lamp stand remained lit for no one. But Waikabubak was at its glorious best during early mornings when dew fell, coating the plants and flowers ready for school.

There was an air of unfriendliness about Waikabubak unlike any other town we had visited in Indonesia. Perhaps it was the heat of the day and its dust. Stony eyes followed us. Greetings were more muted than we expected. And at nights, the broad roads were rumbling with menacing vehicles well past their retirement age followed by the loneliness that set after eight.

But Waikabubak also had its own surprises. On our way to and out of the hotel, we would always meet the gathering of old men at the road corner and distract them from their gossiping. The leader of their group was Uncle Vanya, whose real name was Timo. Timo could speak in broken English and once we told him that we were from Singapore, he used all the good adjectives he knew in English to praise Singapore; "Clean, good, very good, very clean, nice, very very nice." He spoke at such lengths about the greatness of Singapore that it became difficult to have any conversation with him, "Clean, good, very good, very clean, nice, very very nice." It was as if a talking toy that knew the circuit-programmed-words had been set on till its battery died. His wife would stand next to him with admiring looks and like the featuring acts in hip-hop songs, interject periodically, "He knows a lot about Singapore, he is very knowledgeable." Uncle Vanya ran a business of distributing drinking water and there was always a water-vehicle parked near his home looking like a giant red toad.

All sources rambled about the cultural intricacies involved in visiting the traditional villages in Sumba and advised taking a local guide. The manager of Hotel Artha, a guy looking like the legendary Bengali poet, Nazrul Islam, introduced us to one. His name was Daniel, a name rather popular in Sumba. Daniel had intense bloodshot eyes and with his back-brushed hair, hollow features and nasal voice, had an air of instant unlikeability about him, something making him rather unguide-like. It was like a social worker having halitosis. But choices in Waikabubak were few and being Panglossian by nature, we decided to take him on.

Daniel spent the first hour with us explaining why we needed a guide. It was like a salesman making a sales pitch after having already sold something. "There was a Swedish woman who had visited sacred corners in a traditional village alone, without permission, and from then on, walked the streets of Waikabubak stark naked. The police had to put her in prison," he said. Perhaps that was out of fear of destroying the local video rental industry. Daniel thought that unwarranted nudity would be our greatest fear in life and kept on saying, "You need a guide to avoid such things." Then he started on his next big story, "A man in Kodi had a weakness for cigarettes. Guests must enter Sumbanese villages by offering some gifts, cigarettes. Once a tour group entered this man's villages and didn't offer him any cigarettes. So he broke their camera lenses. This could have been easily avoided only if the tour group had gone with a guide. A guide knows every village and every man in these villages. The guide sees a man and knows that he needs cigarettes. The guide sees another man and knows instantly that he doesn't need cigarettes but he is hungry for *sirih pinang*; so he offers him *sirih pinang*." "Travelling in Sumba is possible," said Daniel, "if you only decide to get a guide." I congratulated him for the graciousness of these select people, including himself, who had decided to become guides. In his words, "Life can be beautiful in Sumba for a foreigner. Just take a full package with a guide. Only a few people in Sumba have the character to be a guide. Otherwise, all men in Sumba are NATO. You know what's NATO? No Action, Talking Only. NATO, NATO, NATO. They just love to sit and talk. Not me." Our Carl Linnaeus had established this as the clincher in his sales pitch to tourists and we heard the NATO many times whenever Daniel chased other tourists. "Sumba men only sit on the front porch of their houses all day, chewing *sirih pinang*, spitting out red waste and hoping that *Marapu* will reward them for their laziness. Not me, I wake up at four in the morning, prepare food for my two kids, see them off to school, look for work all the day, then cook dinner and wash clothes."

Daniel was born in Kupang, in West Timor, and then came to Sumba looking for work as many people from Kupang do. He had worked as an English teacher but was now without any permanent employment. He worked on and off as a guide or translator for NGO or Church people. He had married a Sumbanese woman, a health worker, and had helped her build a basic nursing home next to their house to cater to the small health needs of the villagers. With his ever intense look and purposeful voice, it was quite evident that Daniel was not NATO. Over the next week, we saw him ever on the look-out to save a penny, extract a few cents more, look for freebies wherever they were and hoard as much for himself as possible. We coined our own term for people like Daniel - CIA, Constantly Irritating and Annoying.

Daniel was now our guide, "The first thing we should do together as part of our deal is to have lunch." After that, we set about preparing for the village hopping. Daniel bought a handful of *sirih pinang*. While Daniel was negotiating with the old women selling the *sirih pinang* spread out on the road, a man tried to engage us and began teaching us how to chew *sirih pinang*. He pinched me gently here and there, "Get a massage. I am the best," giggling at his innuendos. Of course, it is natural for most people to assume that tourists need a massage whenever possible, but this person seemed to have a natural disposition towards other men. And in front of Lobo, his confidence in his beauty being able to drive me crazy was admirable. He shied away when Daniel came back who promptly started over again his sales pitch on why we need to have a guide, "You know *sirih pinang*? Of course, you don't. How will you know? That's why you need a guide." We told him that we were well familiar with the stuff. He began complaining, "You know nowadays *sirih pinang* is so expensive. I wouldn't make any margin from the price you are paying me for the whole trip." But the cost of *sirih pinang* was a pittance unless Daniel managed his business like a savvy financial trader who could only speak in basis points. To save his margins, he decided that we should walk rather than take a bemo to the first village. "This will give you a good feel of Sumba," he said.

After half an hour of walking under the scorching sun, we finally reached the village of Desa Alu that was not mentioned on any guidebook. Sumbanese villages are usually perched on small hilltops to provide some defence against possible attacks from other clans. Within the village compound, houses are either arranged facing each other, as in most parts around Waikabubak and Anakalang, a district in central Sumba, or in a circular pattern, as is common in Kodi, the westernmost part of the island. These houses have a wooden base, a dug out basement, and giant roofs made of the grass *alang-alang*. These roofs make Sumbanese houses look like Yoda wearing an oversized wizard hat. The central grounds are occupied by megalithic tombs and other paraphernalia dealing with *Marapu*. Practices, customs, language and architecture vary widely from district to district. So while the Kodi houses have the tallest roofs, the Anakalang tombs are the largest.

Till recently, the society in Sumba was divided into castes, nobles, slaves and intermediates. It remains a highly codified society with formal rules of behaviour for most occasions and everyday interactions often interpreted as omens for the future. Sumba also has a long history of internecine conflicts, over cattle, land and slaves. Typically, the men in the island took part in these conflicts but the women also shared the pain and ill-will that came as baggage from these. As such, visiting western parts of Sumba can indeed be a different experience as compared to visiting much of the rest of Indonesia. The day before, we had ventured into a traditional village next to our hotel, behind Uncle Vanya's water bus. We had gone unprepared, like we would visit any other place. While the children had warmed up to us and gave us a big welcome, the village men appeared distant and hesitant to engage with us. There were no approaches, no big hand waves, and no twenty teeth exposure smile to welcome us. Neither did anyone ask the five basic questions any Indonesian asks a tourist, "Where are you from? How many days here? Are you married? Do you have your children? What is your religion?" They just checked on the stickers we gave to the children. Later, we realized that at the least we should have been armed with some *sirih pinang*. Of course, it's not that when we enter a condominium or other such gated complexes anywhere else in the world, adults run to greet us. In super safe Singapore, packs of security guards check on our every life details before letting us enter those fabulous condominium complexes named in French. No friendly stickers or *sirih pinang* would warm them up. But this was Indonesia where seventy five per cent of the people claim to be very happy with life. Incidentally, one senior Indonesian government official once told me that thirty per cent of the population in Indonesia also suffer from some mental problem. I am not sure if this thirty per cent and their families are the ones who make up the seventy five per cent, the super happy people.

As soon as we entered the traditional village Daniel had brought us to, he began stuffing *sirih pinang* into the hands of everyone he came across. The first person we encountered was an old woman who was not able to speak anymore. On receiving the *sirih pinang*, she gave a big, hollow, red stained smile. A few men followed and Daniel gave each a cigarette. Health conscious and globally responsible citizens of the world that we were, there was again a slight feeling of discomfort at handing out these cancerous tubes to innocent villagers just so that we could have a smooth village tour. But our inertia won over our goodwill. There would be no apples and oranges for these villagers, *sirih pinang* and cigarettes it is for them.

As we kept walking, a bunch of men called out for us. Daniel hastily distributed *sirih pinang* and cigarettes to them and some even snatched these from him playfully. They knew Daniel well and we sat with them. They were men of all ages, playing a game of cards. One of the villagers explained, "The loser has to wear a giant earring made of pig's jaw till another person loses. He also has to drink a big bowl of water every time he loses." Women looked on these games from the sides. They offered us tea and the familiar questions followed, "Where are you from? How many days here? Are you married? Do you have your children? What is your religion?"

We were invited to look at the houses. The walls were made of wooden planks and there was a square platform made of bamboo around the floor. As in Flores, the base of the house, under this bamboo flooring, had been dug out for the animals to sleep in. Pigs, chickens and dogs shared this space while the buffaloes were kept in separate enclosures behind the house. The front walls facing the outside were often fully covered with old calendars and posters of movie stars and pop artists.

Roofs of traditional houses in Sumba can be up to ten metres high and are distinct from the ones in Wae Rebo in having rectangular frames. The roof keeps narrowing for up to a height of two metres like a sloping roof after which it rises steeply like an obelisk. The roofing is made of strands of dried grass or *alang-alang*, giving it a particularly shaggy appearance. At the very top of this roof, there is a wooden beam with a male and female idol at each end.

Inside, the house is divided into male and female sections and each has its separate entrance. The kitchen is located at the centre of the house, surrounded by four wooden poles which are very important in Sumbanese culture. One of the poles is dedicated to the clan's religious head or *Rato* for occasional rituals. The other two poles are dedicated to male and female ancestors while the last pole is dedicated to the spirit of fertility. Small sections are marked out inside the room for couples to sleep and for storing objects of religious and ritual importance. One of the villagers explained, "When a couple is trying to have a baby, we put a curtain in their section." Just above the kitchen are the storage chambers where the smoke from the fire helps kill germs and insects. This goes all the way up to the top of the roof from inside. Ladders are made out of cuts within a large bamboo pole.

The families showed us their jewellery boxes; inside which were several pig teeth and *mamuli*, pendants and earrings in traditional design. Like most symbols about tribal life, *mamuli* also represents the male and the female spirit. It looks like an inverted ovary. The male *mamuli* comes with fallopian tube-like structures facing downwards while the female *mamulis* are without such bases. One villager said, "That is why *mamulis* are always given in pairs, one for male and one for female." They hold special importance in rituals because they are usually made of gold and silver, metals once considered divine by the Sumbanese A villager added, "We believe that gold and silver are formed when the sun or the moon set and when shooting stars fall on earth."

The family showed us how they left spaces between the bamboo rods making up the floor so that any leftovers can be thrown to the animals below. Walking on the bamboo floor is not easy for the uninitiated and after taking my first step inside, I slipped and fell back into Lobo's arms like a prince dying in the arms of his princess. Just that, people laughed out loud in this case instead of mourning.

The houses are dark during the day. So, most of the daytime is lived outdoors. At nights, families assemble in houses that have television.

Dreams are invited early and couples practicing procreation muffle their grunts in these houses with no walls within. And all day, pigs and chickens keep looking up from below hoping to receive the crumbs.

The houses are identical in structure but differ in terms of how they are decorated. From a distance, they look like an unorganised herd of brown yaks, brooding in hibernation. Looking closer, their finer details show up. One of the houses had about thirty buffalo skulls placed neatly along the roof for drying. A villager explained, "The owner of this house is a rich man. He is a government official who worked in Java. He had just organised his mother's funeral. It was so lavish."

The ancestral tombs occupy the central grounds of the villages and serve as important landmarks during rituals and feasts. But on normal days, they serve as platforms for drying clothes and shoes. Every such tomb had turned from grey to a patchwork of colours. Since a disproportionate number of residents were children, these clothes were all small sized; a floral bib, a small flabby sack like baby pants, children's sport shoes. Wherever there was some space left on top of the tombs, mother dogs set up vantage points. The fertility pole of the Sumbanese houses does indeed do wonders for the residents whether humans, pigs or dogs. Pups huddled everywhere and pregnant bitches barked incessantly as we walked around. One of the expecting mother dogs came up quietly from behind and tried to bite me. She hit my slippers instead and left neat teeth marks on them.

Daniel asked the village head to bring us the guestbook, part of the ritual of visiting a traditional village. Every village one visits, one has to pay a donation of around ten thousand rupiah per person and then sign in a guest book after writing down name, country and passport number.

The guest book is usually with the *Kepala Kampung*. After all, a village is not the equivalent of a designated attraction like a national park or a monument where the fees are collected for maintaining the site. Houses are supposed to maintain themselves and keep themselves clean for their own sake. But in all fairness, tourists come to Sumba largely to visit these villages. They stay in hotels outside these villages and eat outside as well. Being largely subsistence farmers, the people have little else to offer to tourists for which they can expect a price. Some try to sell ikat but more often than not, visitors are uninterested in buying these. So the only way these poor villagers can make some gain while allowing tourists to visit their homes is to ask for that small donation. And visitors are sparse. The last visitor to Desa Alu had come about four months back. They had to search everywhere to find the guestbook and we realized that it had been used up by children as exercise books. Daniel scolded the villagers for being careless with the guestbook and forced one of the children to sacrifice her new exercise book as the new guest book. "They never take anything seriously," he complained to us.

By now, the villagers and their dogs had become comfortable with us and the *Kepala Kampung* invited us to have another round of tea at his house. The other men left with their pig mandible earring for losers and children joined in to have a closer look at us. The *Kepala Kampung* was a lean man in his sixties, with white beard and deep dark brows. His teeth were stained red and worn off as if he had a habit of biting on the stone tombs. He wore a strange crown, made of tree bark, like Jesus' crown of thorns with a peak at the centre of the forehead. He kept a long knife by his waist, called a *parang*, a custom still followed by most Sumbanese men and he giggled like a young girl. He had got married rather late and had four young children.

Lobo asked him her favourite question, "How did you meet your wife?" He responded slowly, "It had all been arranged by my family. I had to pay a big bride price. When I had gone to propose to my wife's family for the first time, I had to give one buffalo as a gift. Then, during the negotiations, I had to give another five buffaloes and five horses. Finally, at the time of the wedding, I had to give another forty buffaloes in addition to some land and gold and silver ornaments." This was back-breaking even by Sumbanese standards and the Kepala Kampung indeed walked with a hunch. I told them that in most parts of India, it was the bride's family who had to pay a hefty price to the groom. And if the bride's family didn't pay the agreed amount, she could be tortured to the point of being burnt. In my broken Bahasa Indonesia, I explained this brutal act as "Istri bakar" or grilling the wife, at which the traditional village with its peaked husky roofs broke into rolling laughter. The *Kepala Kampung* just covered his mouth and giggled, his head bobbing like an excited pigeon. He was a Jimmy Carter of a *Kepala Kampung*.

The children were playing with the giant horns of a buffalo skull that adorned the front of his house. They began to kick us gently to ask to take their photographs. Slowly they would come over my ears and whisper, "*Mau Foto*," or "I want photo". At the house of the *Kepala Kampung* in Desa Alu, they were the nobility and I was the slave class.

We moved on to the next village of Waitabar. Outside the rough and dusty roads of Waikabubak, highland Sumba was a pleasant green of rice fields and dwarf hills. Geckos ran from our path, scrambling to draw in their long tails. The village of Waitabar is located right next to another, Tarung. These twins were, as typical of Sumba, located on a hill, whose trails were guarded by giant stone horses. At Waitabar, the village women slowly assembled around us, holding to their chest, spread out ikat. Daniel had prepared us before for this and we had memorized our lines, "Thank you, sorry, thank you, sorry, we are just looking around, not looking to buy anything. These are very nice, but thank you, sorry, thank you, sorry." It worked and the women slowly dispersed to the husky houses in the evening light.

However, I increasingly felt empowered whenever I was approached with ikat. For Sumba is the only bastion of men's fashion in a world where men's clothing come in as many variations as crude oil. In Sumba, where unlike women who wear relatively simple ikat skirts, a man may wear ikat as shoulder cloth, sarong, turban and waist band. The patterns in the men's ikat are not to be taken lightly, for they tell much about the person's social standing. The most expensive ikat are given to the groom as a return gift for the bride-price. The glory is hallowed by the fact that only women are involved in ikat making, a skill that adds several points to her CV as a worthy bride. She can take no shortcuts and often has to wait for weeks for that perfect berry to blossom in that faraway vine to get the colour her man must wear. And the mystery and the suspense around the fall winter collection are enhanced by the practice of forbidding men to be anywhere near the dye making process. As for accessories, add a *mamuli* to the man's ear, a machete in an elegantly carved case of buffalo horn by the waist, and of course, some red stained teeth. Oh, I love Sumba, if only for imagining that I could be a Bird of Paradise here.

The *Kepala Kampung* was not around in Waitabar and Daniel quipped that there was no point wasting donation money on this village and we should move on. But families idling outside their homes called us and offered us *sirih pinang*.

Sumba saying: Don't ever refuse *Sirih Pinang*.

So both Lobo and I accepted their kind offer and painted the world red with our spit. Lobo immediately felt intoxicated and the women of the village rushed to offer her sweet warm water as we laughed heartily at her travails.

Sumba saying: Eternal bonds are formed when you chew *sirih pinang* together.

The villagers pointed to an older man in the village, perhaps in his eighties or nineties, who despite having lost all his teeth, still couldn't get rid of his love for *sirih pinang*. "He spends his whole day grinding the *sirih pinang* into a paste." We felt bad about our plan to save on the donation money. After all, these villagers just wanted a good laugh and an opportunity to engage with the outside world. But Daniel was chasing us, "There is nothing interesting about this village."

At the village of Tarung, we met Julianne, a woman in her thirties. She was weaving an ikat scarf and asked us to sit down and have tea with her and her friends who had assembled at her house. The front wall of Sumbanese houses are precious real estate. That's the only visible place where anything the resident family wants to display to boast about, can be showcased. Some put massive buffalo horns while some put a framed copy of their college degrees if they have one. Julianne had put a small framed picture of her with a Caucasian woman. Around the white border of the picture, was written in big fonts, "Taken in Paris". Julianne had been working in a restaurant in Bali before and over there, she also taught Bahasa Indonesia to foreigners. She came across a French man to whom she got married and had a daughter with. She had stayed in Paris for a few months after which she and her daughter came back to their family house in Tarung. She, together with her old mother, was now the breadwinner of the household and made a living by selling ikat. "Business is good," she said, "The local police department has recently given a massive order of ikat scarfs for their annual bash." The scarfs bore the name of the department, "Bhayankara", which in most languages derived from Sanskrit meant dangerous or deadly. When I told this to the gathering, they said, "That seems like an appropriate name for the police department." Julianne's daughter came out and it was obvious that she was the star of the household, adored by everybody. She had green eyes, straight hair and a facial structure that showed that she was of mixed race. Only six years old, she had also emerged as the leader of the kids in the village, directing them on what to do and how to behave. She had taught a kitten to kiss and made fun of me when I called it *Pipin,* one of the characters of the famous Malaysian cartoon series *Ipin* and *Upin.* She was flipping through her books and was startled to see a picture of a pink *Ikan Paus* or whale. "How can an *ikan paus* be pink?" she asked us all in Bahasa Indonesia. The discussion veered back to our identities and once again, I became the representative for Bollywood to Indonesia. This job, although it came with a lot of responsibility, was relatively easy for me, even though the last Bollywood movie that I had watched was perhaps a good fourteen years ago. The villagers would take names of the stars, movies and songs randomly and I could pass just by repeating them or smiling at them with a know-it-all look. One girl remarked, "Sharukh Khan," and I would repeat, "Ya, Shahrukh Khan." "*Kuch kuch hota hai,*"

Julianne interjected, and I would smile and say, "that's right, Ya, *Kuch kuch hota hai*." Another young girl would then take a long name which I had never heard of and I would just smile and raise my brows, "How do you all know so much?" That's all I had to do as part of representing India and Bollywood to Indonesia.

There was no theatre in West Sumba so Julianne and her gang relied on DVDs and the radio for their dose of Bollywood. Julianne herself had been some kind of star when she was featured in a Survivor-like television series in Indonesia. "I had come back to Sumba to make sure that our daughter grew up in the Sumbanese way and not the Western way," Julianne told us. She herself spoke English and French fluently but her daughter spoke only Bahasa Indonesia. Though I could admire Julianne, she confused me. She had a lot more control of her life than any other women I had met in these traditional villages. She must have missed Sumba enough to leave the temptations of the West and even Bali. But why was then the emphasis of "Taken in Paris" on the wall photograph? Later Daniel put in his own version, "No one knows why she came back? No one knows if she was even married to that white guy. Sometimes young people just enjoy." But then that was Daniel who probably saw the world as a constant conflict between self-interests. As we prepared to leave, Julianne shouted at us, "Excuse me, one last question, what language do you and Lobo use to speak to each other?"

We were left with a sweet after-taste after visiting these three villages of Desa Alu, Waitabar, and Tarung. Men with machetes had seemed friendly. Women holding ikat to their chests seemed more eager to know about us than making a sale. Daniel was exuberant as he eagerly gulped down his dinner on our account, "This is why you need a guide. You can sit down with the Kepala Kampung and talk and know more about them. There is no better way to travel. With me, you have no fear. I know what makes them happy. Last year, one Swiss tourist didn't have a guide and then ...."

But these villages could easily become grounds for bloody mass violence. In 1998, this was over a nickname. A few months after Suharto's exit, people from the Loli tribe had been protesting against corruption attributed to the *bupati* or regent of West Sumba. One of his nephews had apparently passed a civil services exam without even taking it. During demonstrations outside the *bupati's* home, the Loli people had apparently chanted his nickname. This was seriously improper in the Sumbanese context. Every traditional Sumbanese name has a fixed nickname associated with it that can only be used by relatives or close friends in certain established contexts. Infusriated, the Weweqa tribe, to which the *bupati* belonged, assembled three thousand fellow tribesmen from the nearby highlands to take revenge. They came with machetes, rocks, spears, wooden clubs and bundles of dried grass to set Lolo houses on fire. They marched towards Tarung, the most important village for the Loli tribe. The Loli people threw rocks and sharp objects at them from the hills they occupied. The Wewewans threw up balls of fire to cook the stars. The Loli people were fewer but they held on. The spears of the Loli split into four as they went down looking for Wewewa blood. Rocks loosened themselves from the hills and rushed towards the Wewewa taking their own revenge for breaking the silence. That's what the people of Tarung say. And then the rains appeared, unexpectedly, and washed away any Wewewa hopes of burning Loli roofs. The battle ceased. The police recorded death in the high twenties. Peace was finally restored two weeks later when according to tradition, leaders of the two communities gathered in a purpose-built house near the battlefield to talk. Ritual songs in Loli and Wewewa languages were sung, buffaloes and pigs were exchanged, and vows were taken by the respective leaders to forgive and forget.

Such battles have been common in Sumba. Much of the eighteenth and nineteenth century saw tribal wars to acquire slaves for their own use as well as for selling to the wider world. Fighting to get land, stone quarries for tombs, water buffaloes, and horses were also common. Even now in Kodi, the district at the westernmost and poorest corner of Sumba, where much of the population still rely on the dry method for cultivation of rice, fast loss of fertility of the soil means that fights are still frequent among different clans.

Traditional Sumbanese society is highly codified, somewhat akin to the Chinese, perhaps even more so. There are rules for every aspect of life. Greeting with *sirih pinang* and avoiding nicknames in public settings are only some of the instances. So for some, every gesture has a meaning as does the intestine of every chicken that is slaughtered. Which way the wind blows is as loaded with symbolism as what colour the calves of the buffaloes are. And while the atmosphere is extremely civil towards foreigners like us, in such a rigid ritualized way of living, deviations and the resulting disappointments come thick and easy. Why didn't my brother in law give as many buffaloes during my mother's funeral as he was supposed to? Why is he building a second tomb when he already has one? Why did she pretend to be sick when I asked her for help in planting rice at our fields? Why did so few sea worms turn up on the eighth day after full moon, will we have the worst harvest of our lives?

The situation is especially intense in Kodi and over there even tourists haven't been spared an occasional punch or two. When we visited the weekly market in the small town of Kori, in Kodi district, blank stares followed us. The market was hot and dusty, heavy from the smell of dried fish. Sellers were squatting, many of them old women who understood no Bahasa Indonesia. Men with no purpose were standing at the fringes, machetes jutting from their waists. No one was buying anything and the sellers were getting edgy with each person walking away. Daniel asked us to stay close to him but he got distracted when he saw a peanut seller. Under the pretext of having a taste, he ate a lot. We were worried that he might get beaten up. Young boys were walking around with wooden crates tied to their necks, selling medicines. "Ampicillin, ampicillin, Aspirin, aspirin", they were whispering like dragons in the hot air. These boys were waiting for a fight to break out so that they could be the paramedic heroes. This was the biggest market in Kodi region but there was little on display. The region was indeed poor.

But despite Kodi's rough reputation, in it nestles a small side story of an immense capacity to love. In the village of Wainyapu, the village head has created a legend of his virility by having over a dozen wives. This has brought him international fame and he is a popular totem to visit for male tourists seeking an inspiration. We skipped visiting him, not wanting him to burden with another volley of questions that must be all too familiar to him, "How do you manage? How do your wives get along?" and then the whisper, "Come, tell me the secrets of your power?"

By the time we reached Ratenggaro, a traditional village along the Kodi coast, we were already suffering from village-visiting-fatigue. We walked in, paid the donation money, refused to buy the handicrafts, quickly handed out a few stickers to the kids, walked around to take pictures, avoided much conversation with the local *Kepala Kampung*, and rushed out on our motorbikes; the children running behind us asking for some more stickers and money. This, despite Ratenggaro having a very legitimate claim for being the most beautiful village in the world. Its houses were neatly arranged in a circle. As is typical of Kodi, the roofs were much taller than one can see in rest of Sumba. They were also more trimmed than the unruly husky ensembles in other Sumba villages and were of lighter colour, mirroring the sun. That's because they were relatively new, built after a devastating fire.

In the neatly trimmed lawn at the centre of the village, the white cows and baby horses drinking milk from their mothers added more idealism to the pastoral ideal. And the village was perched above the vast sea that bent in like a giant ring in front of the village encircling an oval shaped sand bar. The sea ring had turned turquoise under a clear blue sky and the sand bar glittered and glittered and glittered. A handful of ornately curved megalithic tombs from ancient times guarded the village from the sea. This was a perfect place for lying dead as this was also the end of the world; for if one draws a line west, there won't be land till Africa.

But as for the villagers, we had heard their stories many times. Houses burnt every now and then; at Ratenggaro, the entire village had been burned down eight years back from an accidental fire and they were yet to rebuild the place completely. Recurring stories of giving buffaloes and pigs for every special occasion that kept people on a continuous cycle of debt and impoverishment; the spirit of *Marapu* and the sacrifices it demands from time to time, the endless chewing of *sirih pinang*, the donation book, the handing over of cigarettes, could life be any different in Sumba? Were tourists like us paying these villagers to remain the way they were, always in fear of nature and everyone outside their clan, building photogenic but impractical houses? Perhaps not, because after all there were so few tourists in Sumba.

We followed the same photo-hungry strategy in another village near Marosi located in Lamboya district, south western Sumba. We didn't even bother to ask the name of the village. Daniel had probably sensed our revulsion of him by now and left us to roam around the village on our own while he chatted with the *Kepala Kampung*. Angry dogs surrounded us till we picked pebbles to show we had deterrence. Men walked around holding machetes, looking at us without the usual smile. Two of them came up to us to ask for cigarettes. We ran back to Daniel and he gave us an uplifting speech, "Don't give them anything. It's pitiful. They are behaving like beggars. Tell them we have already paid the donation." We sought succour with the children who regarded our gift of stickers as a good enough gesture of friendship. They took us to a mother pig that had just given birth to quintuplets that looked more like baby monkeys with their folded joints, scraggy frames and swirling tails. They took us to a girl in her late teens who could talk to chickens. She picked them up and threw them away and when she called them out in her strange way, they came back to her to be lifted up again. She asked us to try her approach. I was cuddling an adult chicken for the first time and its warm touch, the feel of its ribs and the heartbeat, and the stare straight into my eyes, made me feel like I was holding an alien baby, very fragile who might get crushed from a little more careless pressure from my fingers, but still trusting me hesitantly. Of course, they didn't come back to us when we dropped them like the girl had advised, so we offered her stickers so she would teach us the spell. She hid her face with her arms, giggling.

On our way back, Daniel pointed to a resort. "That's what all foreigners and NGOs do in Sumba," said Daniel, "they are all looking for land to build hotels where they can charge four hundred dollars a night. We can't even go to the beaches by those hotels. The villagers get nothing from these people." But Daniel had come to rely on these very people for his livelihood.

By now, we had been thoroughly tired of Daniel and were using him mainly as an ojek driver, avoiding him as soon as we reached the places of interest. Instead of talking about the culture of the place, he kept talking about the low margins in his business as a guide. He would take us to far fewer places than he would commit at the beginning of each day. Sometimes, when we bought snacks or drinks for him and the other ojek driver he had hired, he would do silly things to keep them for himself. Whenever he saw us handing out stickers, he would say, "There is no need to give them anything. Give me all these stickers for my kids." His nasal voice was piercing our ears and triggering the hatred cortex in our brains. And he would look for every excuse to get a few dollars more. Even though it was he who was planning our schedule, he would say, "I had already prepared lunch for you at my home. This will now be wasted because we have travelled so far away." At Kodi, where his in-laws resided, he said that there were no *warungs* or small restaurants and we should eat at their in-laws' house instead, "It would be a great opportunity for you to visit a non-traditional Sumba home," he said, "You can just make a small donation to let my in-laws know of your appreciation." By now, quite familiar with his schemes, I asked him how much the cost would be and he quoted fifteen dollars. When I said we plan to skip lunch, he dropped the price to five dollars but later made it up by just offering rice and soup. We drove past many *warungs* to his in-laws house. There, he didn't seem to be very welcome. We were seated outside, behind the house. Daniel's father-in-law asked Lobo when she walked past him to use their toilet, "Did you bring *sirih pinang?*" His mother, a very old woman, perhaps not fully in her senses by now, came over to us, "Tobacco?" Two very skinny dogs followed with sorrowful eyes. For the first time in Sumba, we met humble dogs and we joked with Yonus, the other ojek driver, that given how penny-pinching Daniel and his family seemed to be, it was only natural for these poor dogs to live a famished life. They gratefully finished the food we gave them till Daniel came and shooed them away. We had paid Daniel already our token of appreciation which he had asked in advance so he could do the necessary shopping for our meal. But at this point, he began asking for some small money, in front of his in-laws, "Maybe three or five dollars to show your appreciation?" We said we didn't have any more money, and asked him to go straight to our hotel so that we didn't have to deal with him anymore. On the way, I asked him how he had turned out to be such an exception to Indonesian civility. He didn't seem to understand and kept on messaging and calling me over the next two days offering trips to this village or that. By then, we had already left Sumba.

But besides Daniel and the routine of travelling with him, Sumba was getting more familiar and delightful by the day. The landscape didn't have the apocalyptic serenity of the famous volcanoes of Java and Flores, or the tedious familiarity of orangutan forests in Sumatra and Kalimantan, but it had enough to charm our minds. While Sumba is relatively dry compared to the rest of Indonesia, lush hills and rice plantations cover much of the south-west part of the island. Muddy rivers wind lazily. Bare-breasted old ladies walked by with humped backs. Young boys galloped in horses over red harvest-ready fields to get stickers from us. At Pero, lonely fisherman stood on cliffs to catch the mighty waves with their makeshift fishing rods. Alligator-nosed rocks jut out over those turquoise seas, attracting buffaloes and cows to watch the whirlpools forming under them. Young boys, managers of these herds, sat down with us to picnic over biscuits and then showed some daredevilry, somersaulting over buffalo backs, sliding over their backs, diving under their legs; the buffaloes standing frozen in bewilderment.

It was here, in Pero, that I set a trap for Daniel who had gone away to buy groceries for our lunch at his in-laws. After finishing the biscuits and groundnuts, I spread out their empty packages in front of us as bait. I was sure that Daniel with his go-grab-it attitude will fall for it while Lobo and Yonus were more circumspect. But the moment he came back, without saying a word, Daniel frisked through the packages, one by one. We could barely control our laughter when he went through each of the groundnut shells hoping to salvage something.

The sea and the sand flirted with each other for long stretches at Pantai Marosi and Pantai Rua, tiny transparent crabs running from one to the other trying to make peace between the two. The road to Marosi beach is kerbed by young women with black buckets over their heads. They walked slowly on both sides of the road, swaying gently. The buckets on the way to the beach are empty; the ones coming back are filled with sea-weed which they use for cooking.

Even Waikabubak, which had seemed unwelcoming from first experiences, had turned up its own platter of friends for us. We looked forward to evenings, when Daniel would leave us, and we would be on our own, checking on these friends. One of them was the owner of a small grocery store, a gentle man called Martin. Martin was very skinny with a moustache too big for his face. He was also from Kupang like Daniel but his exact opposite. Every evening, we would buy some bread from him to make up for the meagre hotel breakfast. And every day, he would advise us, "Careful, children. Don't stay out too late. You are strangers here." Martin's shop had only sweet knick-knacks, sweet cakes, sweet bread, chocolates, sweet drinks and sweet biscuits. He said that these were bought by the army people whose dormitories were just behind his shop. He had been in the army himself, "Army men love sweet things." But Martin's shop was also right opposite a Surabaya hair salon run by a bunch of ladyboys. Could it have been them who made Martin store only these sweet things? It was hard to tell because we never saw any other customer in Martin's shop. Perhaps he had already convinced everyone to stay away from these dark lonely streets at those late hours, eight at night.

We had also made friends with Joko, a character who had come to Waikabubak from central Java to set up a gloriously titled "Warung Arabia" that sold grilled chicken, soup and STMJ, an acronym for the popular Indonesian drink *Susu Telur Madu Jahe* or Milk, Egg, Honey and Ginger. Joko was in his thirties, rather stocky, dark in complexion, with trimmed moustache and a thin ponytail. He wore a FC Barcelona t-shirt every day. The teenage boy who grilled the chicken for him had been also hired from Java. He looked like a Japanese manga legend, with sharp streaks of hair running over a brown metallic face. He tossed and turned the chicken with exaggerated movements accompanied by whistles imitating aerial dog-fights. Joko's *warung* was ever popular and it was tough to get a place. The next day after we first got to know his place, we asked a man at another restaurant for the way to Warung Arabia. Rather shyly, he said, "My restaurant is also called Warung Arabia. But the original one is over there." The food had indeed delighted Lobo and she ate more than her usual habit at Joko's place. He had a few pictures of one celebrity visiting his *warung* and then visiting his home with his wife. The oil from the non-stop grilling had turned the pictures grimy. We asked Joko to replace the grimy celebrity pictures with ours for we were bigger celebrities than the one he had on now. Joko gave out his customary laughter, a sound of muffled machine gun fire but perhaps saw logic in this. He didn't have a camera so we agreed to take a picture for him and then mail it over. But when I posed with the plate of chicken, Joko, an otherwise boisterous spirit, couldn't help looking nervous. We tried a few times but he remained stiff on all occasions. And I was looking so dishevelled from all the travel that it was hard to identify the celebrity between me and Joko.

With Joko, food was becoming less of an issue in Waikabubak. We also began discovering semi-precious gems, a street vendor selling layers of warm bread filled with cheese and condensed milk, a powerful concoction that once eaten, immediately formed layers of fat inside the body. And there was Bubu, the young boy managing the fried banana stall with his father, who had taken the more menial job of cooking the bananas in the big oil bath. Once, stung by sand flies, we went to ask Bubu for used banana skins. He gave us a big bright smile, searched among the waste for the best banana skins, cleaned them and gave them to us. Sand flies, sand flies, protectors of the sea!

The most enigmatic of the Waikabubak characters was Steve, a sixty-something man, dark and skinny with hollowed out cheeks. He always wore a Singapore army uniform and a cap with the name J.L. Chua written on it. He hung around the hotel trying to sell handicrafts which he carried around in his various pockets. Some elongated items, like carved machete cases; he just put inside his sleeves. Steve also wore several bands and strings around his wrist. Whenever Steve saw us, he would ask a few questions, "Where did you go? What will you do now? Do you need a machete?" Whatever we replied, he would always break into a giggle; a long, rippling giggle. Sometimes he giggled just at our sight. Steve knew the meaning of life.

For him, we were too tiny particles of the universe, too insignificant, living life by rules we didn't know who set and why, and he couldn't help laughing at us. Whatever we did or whatever we intended to do was utterly silly for him. But he was full of compassion and didn't insult us for our petty existence. It's just that once you know the infinite, it's hard to control laughter at the ants. Steve was the reincarnation of Kurt Vonnegut.

Everyone else said that Steve had lost his mind. His wife had run away with another man when she had found out his true sexual preferences. It was not clear what role J.L. Chua had played in all this. Steve never cried. Instead, he used his abilities to provide massage to tourists. And he spoke the best English in Waikabubak. Daniel couldn't stand Steve and would disappear whenever Steve was around. We loved Steve for that and but for his dirty uniform, I felt like hugging him every time we came back to the hotel after a long day with Daniel. With his healing voice, Steve would immediately return us back our souls. One day, we wanted to take his picture but he was adamant in not posing by himself. So Lobo stood by him and Steve asked me to capture all the wrist bands he was wearing. When we were leaving, Steve was first surprised and then he became very sad, "Why?" It was as if he would now have to report this development to someone superior who might question him for his ignorance. But soon, he regained his composure and his giggle rose above the motorcycle din.

Lobo had also made her own set of friends with her unique style, by asking for toilets. Many times in Waikabubak, as we took a stroll in its lonely dark streets, I would have to knock on doors to ask if Lobo could use their toilets. I was just playing the role of the twenty-first century man, full of chivalry and courage. Invariably, the residents would invite us in very graciously. The woman of the house would lead Lobo somewhere, past the bedrooms and kitchen, while I would be invited for a cup of tea by the male host. Later, Lobo would tell me, "This is how their house looks like." Once we chanced upon an antique dealer's home who had made a small fortune by selling antiques to shops in Bali. His house, rather simple from outside, had intricately curved furniture inside. Once we entered the home of a restaurant owner whose domestic helpers searched for a long time to find the lady of the house. Once she came, she started behaving like a Japanese hostess, with her ever-bent back, asking us to forgive the mess in her grand home. At times, these niceties on their part would be a little over the top for all we needed was a toilet for Lobo.

The list of warm gestures kept piling up. At the bank, a security guard asked me to take off my cap for security reasons and then felt rather guilty for it. He tried to make up for it by becoming a constant companion and accompanied me to the photocopy shop where he even offered to pay. At Pantai Rua, where the *bupati* had come on an event to showcase local economic activity, we stole his thunder. The participants leaned over one another to ask us to sample their wares, a unique sweet drink with loads of ginger, various cookies, even raw vegetables. A group of middle-aged women who had just given a traditional dance performance came running to us to take pictures along with us. They were still sweating profusely because the podium was not under any shade. They were all government employees and selected the junior-most among them to take our pictures. So many people handed their cameras and phones to her that the poor girl became a Christmas tree of dangling lenses. Women took pictures, first with their glasses on, then without glasses, once with the 'friends' sign, once with a thumbs up. The only man among them also joined the fray but he wanted to take pictures only with Lobo for which he was well talked about behind his back. A doctor who was walking around in his uniform and stethoscopes also approached us offering to do a quick health check for us. At this point, Daniel, taken aback with such effusion of friendly gestures, that too without a guide's aid, drove them away and took us away. He might have later asked the *bupati* for a medal.

Then there were the ones living their lives in these islands, whose names we forgot to ask. At Wanokaka, we had lunch at a small *warung* run by an old couple. The man was from Flores and had come to Sumba as a teacher and then got married to a local woman. Other patrons at the *warung* told us that they were a very smart couple who had done well for themselves and also for the village. But when it came to giving us change, the poor man messed up his maths and gave us a lot more back than was due. We caught the other patrons giggling when we were correcting the mistake. Perhaps that's what these men meant when they said the couple had done well for the village.

In Sumba, we came across several young men who were working somewhere else in Indonesia and had come back to help their communities during the harvest period. Most of them worked in Bali, in jobs linked to tourism, hoping to learn English in the process. Some went with their wives who also found a job there but most didn't see their families for months. Perched on a hilltop before Waikabubak, overlooking the perfect greenery of rice fields and coconut palms, we came across a lonely house full of chickens and their hatchlings and a mother dog with four puppies. There was an old woman residing there and her son wouldn't come back this year from Bali. But the chicks and puppies gave her good company, coming to her and following her whenever she stepped on the grounds.

On the way from Marosi to Waikabubak, we came across a *Dangdut* party, a very Indonesian invention that came somewhere between a Roman orgy and a night club. This *Dangdut* party was happening in a small house with mud floors and thatched roofs, just after lunch hours. The music was blaring and a young woman with cropped hair, loud makeup and PVC clothing was dancing in the centre with exaggerated hip thrusts, appearing in a state of trance. The audience comprised of a few disinterested young men and women, perhaps couples. Outside this room, a young man with round features was standing guard. He told us that he was on parole and a case was going on against him for murdering his village head. "He had insulted my family," he said, "He lent us some money at very bad rates." He seemed rather harmless, one of those many Indonesian faces that don't seem to harbour any spirit to fight back at anything. But he was surprisingly careless in admitting his offence to any stranger passing by. Perhaps, it was a ploy by the *Dangdut* organisers to keep off local Islamists for whom *Dangdut* was intolerable.

Just outside a girl's school at Lamboya Pasola fields, we met a plump young woman selling ice candies. She was a beehive surrounded by millions of girl bees in uniform. She had come from Sumbawa with her husband, a Sumbanese who once worked at Sumbawa. When the couple had come back to his ancestral home in Sumba, they had tried to set up a *warung* but business came to nothing outside of the *Pasola* season, the annual mock fight festival in Sumba. Now the husband was out of work and the woman had to make ends meet by selling these sweet nothings. She had great sadness in her eyes for a beehive. But the bees around her were in a state of perpetual excitement.

On the *Pasola* fields in front of us, hundreds of buffaloes were grazing contentedly, keeping the fields trimmed for the next year's event. During *Pasola*, two teams, drawn from different villages confront each other. Men dressed in traditional garb, riding horses, gallop towards opponents, throwing blunt wooden spears. The fights are usually stopped when blood spills for the first time, an event considered auspicious for the coming harvest. Several rituals precede the *Pasola*.

Around February or March, following cues from the phases of the moon, elders scan the seas for the germination of a certain kind of sea worm. The dates for the *Pasola* are accordingly set. The *Pasolas* begin around the coasts and are then followed by *Pasolas* inland.

On the day of the *Pasola*, entire clans, men and women, young and old, assemble around the grounds and surrounding hilltops to cheer their teams. Police come around in big numbers to prevent things getting out of control although locals say that they abuse their power to get the best views. Each fighting man carries a handful of spears and within minutes of commencement, the fields become a valley of fallen spears. Teams deploy special units to collect them and bring them back to the warriors. Locals excitedly talk about many deaths in recent events but in reality, there has probably not been any over the last few years, though injuries are common. Death of horses are also possible during these events as many frequently trip and fall or get skull damage from the spears. One man told us, "A person gets hurt or killed only if he has a bad character. If someone is pure at heart, nothing can happen to him during the *Pasola*." At the same time, some people call on magical powers of the *Marapu* to inflict harm on others during the event.

Every village has its own *Pasola* heroes and their legends, often middle-aged men, who would recall in detail how many men he had downed and how that whole moment transpired. In present days, the *Pasola* defines Sumba for the rest of the world. These fights are telecast live all over Indonesia and even to Malaysia. Hotels fill up and several new *warungs* crop up out of nowhere around the *Pasola* fields.

Sumba also has a sizeable population of people of Chinese and Indian origin. The Indians are far fewer but their numbers have increased recently as they began coming in as traders in cashew nuts. Many of these traders stayed in Sumba only for a few months though. The photocopy shop next to the bank was run by an Indian lady who had come to Sumba fifty years ago with her husband, a trader. She was rather less excited to meet me than the friendly security guard who took me there and was delighted to get me to meet another Indian.

As for the Chinese, they were far more numerous, usually controlling the visibly more prosperous parts of the economy in both Flores and Sumba. At both these islands, the Chinese would run the biggest stores, the better-looking restaurants, and most of the hotels. In many of the towns, these would be clustered together. So in Waikabubak, there were five general stores, all looking the same, next to each other. Next to them was a hotel run by a Chinese family. That they all looked the same was not strange, because they all traced their origin to the same ancestor. These Chinese stores looked very different from the *warungs*, much larger, with high roofs, lots of glass casings everywhere, and bright fluorescent lights instead of the tiny incandescent bulbs in the *warungs*.

The Chinese have been in Indonesia for hundreds of years, as traders, never liked, often called 'leeches' for their aggressive terms of trade for dealing with the locals. This resentment against their squeeze, their visible wealth, fairer women, and different religion, led to several killings, rapes and other gentler forms of violence on the Chinese after independence, the greatest of which were during the takeover by Suharto in 1965 and the fall of Suharto in 1998.

After Indonesian independence, the Chinese were victimised for different, often contradictory reasons. After the takeover of Beijing by the People's Army, the Indonesian Chinese were often suspected of being closet communists, godless and ever ready to shift loyalties to the new China. But reality was that the Indonesian Chinese, most of who came from Southern Coastal provinces as traders, had little to benefit from Marxist ideology. If the Indonesian communist party had come to power after Sukarno and adopted their professed redistribution policies, the Chinese would have stood to lose the most in terms of material wealth and economic potential. Instead, during the slaughter of communist party members in Indonesia during the Suharto takeover that eventually led to the wipe-out of the world's largest communist party, the Chinese were also identified as natural targets. And while Suharto's regime followed a policy of forced assimilation of the Chinese through banning of Chinese names, Chinese language education, and Chinese festivals and rituals; during this period, the Chinese actually consolidated their economic power to a much greater extent, either through bribery or by paying security money to all levels at community and government. So while the launch of the Suharto regime was seen by the majority as the beginning of the end of Chinese economic dominance, the end of his regime was also being seen by the majority as the beginning of the end of the same Chinese dominance. Only after the mass killings and rape of Chinese during the unrest of 1998, did the Indonesian government gradually allow certain rights to the Chinese. They were now free to use their language and Chinese festivals can now be openly celebrated.

But something had been lost. Lobo couldn't talk to most of the Chinese we came across and I had to be the interlocutor in Bahasa Indonesia between the two. While only the older generation still knew how to speak in the Hokkien dialect, those born after the sixties had no use of the Chinese language. At a grocery store, one of those grander stores in Waikabubak, the middle-aged owner struggled to explain the meaning of his Chinese name. Lobo translated it as honesty, integrity and strength but I, with a limited vocabulary of Bahasa Indonesia, struggled to explain these words to the man. Finally, I gave up and said that he had the best name possible in the world, *'nama paling baik',* and that reassured both Lobo and the man. Another Hokkien-speaking old man, who ran a large pharmacy, insisted that a majority of Indians also spoke Mandarin.

In Sumba and Flores, the Chinese had been exposed to less of the violence and everyone we spoke with said that things were fine now and they didn't face any problems. But both Lobo and I noticed that most of them had lost their ability to smile. Lobo, a mainland Chinese herself, was getting more and more furious with all such interactions. Not only was she disappointed with the relatively bland southern Chinese food at the restaurants hyped by locals as the best in every town we visited; she also thought that their conversations were never warm and always trying to establish the social standing of the other person. She would in particular get angry thinking that the local Chinese frowned when they got to know that Lobo and I were about to get married. Much richer than the locals, but unable to be happy, to smile, and to open up to others; that's what Lobo thought of them.

But then we met Theresa May, the only Chinese woman who had participated in the *Bupati* event at Pantai Rua. She was so delighted to meet Lobo that she kept on hugging her and patting her cheeks, calling her a younger sister. She took many pictures with us and invited us to her house at Waikabubak. She and her family ran one of the big general stores and her husband, possibly a good twenty years older than her, appeared to be an equally jovial person. They smiled and smiled, and when we were about to leave, began stocking up a bag for us with varieties of food from their store. We had to take out most of the things out of fear that their business would go into the red as a result of this generosity. Just when we were well on our way to forming stereotypes, life continued to surprise us.

So this was Sumba. Beyond the machetes around the waist, ever ready to kill and the donation mindset at some villages, there was an overtly friendly side, extending eager arms to the rest of the world. But while we like to say that people everywhere have the same concerns, money, health, social standing; in Sumba, the obsession with death distinguished its culture. So when Daniel informed us that a death had occurred in a nearby village, we were delighted! The deceased was the mother of a rich man. Even better news, for greater wealth meant greater ritual displays and bigger tombs! We waited eagerly for the next day.

Close encounters of the death kind

In a society, where ancestors are revered a lot more than living beings, death is the moment when a man or woman finally gets his or her moment of glory. Death is after all the point of escape from the world of common insignificance to the elevated world of *Marapu*, a few steps closer to God. So people spend great fortunes to build tombs and organise feasts to commemorate the burials. It is also the moment when social ties are audited again by evaluating the gifts received from relatives and friends. It is the most important opportunity for the households to announce their social standing and therefore is not to be taken lightly. The grander the tomb and the ceremonies, the stronger the message sent about the household's social standing.

While the huge expenses related to death may seem pointless to other cultures, in the Sumbanese context, there are very practical reasons for defining life by the way of handling death. For instance, the message of social standing sent through the opulence of the burials has obvious implications for the marriage prospects of the next generation. Many households toil for years to assemble the necessary financial resources while the dead body is buried in a simple grave close to the house while the family saves for the big tomb and ceremony. Families often incur massive debts in the process. While this would often result in slavery in the recent past; in present times, the situation can be only slightly better for the indebted. So when a funeral is announced, it becomes the biggest news in the community and surrounding villages. Two such ceremonies were to happen around Waikabubak within the next four weeks and the town was abuzz with this.

Sumbanese tombs look like stone vaults with four walls and a tabletop. The stone at the top is often decorated with carvings of buffalo head and its posterior as well as *mamuli*. Some have the buffalo head at one end and a cross at the other. A tomb may be shared by many family members but incest taboo is enforced strictly. So the dead children can never be kept together with their parent's bodies, while it is possible to bury them together with grandparents. It is also common for the rich and mighty to build tombs for themselves in advance.

All along western Sumba, one can see megalithic tombs, some dating to over five hundred years ago, with patches of algae growth over them. In the Anakalang region, at the centre of Sumba, the tombs are the biggest, while in Kodi, the tombs are relatively smaller. This difference has often been ascribed to the relative prosperity of Anakalang where wet rice cultivation has been practised for centuries unlike Kodi where dry rice cultivation is still the rule.

The process of building a tomb can take more than a decade as families wait to save up or borrow enough to build one. It is quite common to give up half way and continue from where one had left after a few years when enough money has been accumulated. The process of building a tomb involves the entire community as well as specialists from outside if required and as such, one has to first seek permission from the entire community before launching such a massive project. If a household has already built a tomb and is seeking approval for building a second one, they may be overridden, especially if another household is already waiting to build their first tomb. Animals are usually sacrificed during this approval-seeking process and small feasts organised for the entire village. Once the permission has been obtained, the stones have to be bought from the handful of sandstone quarries that exist in Sumba. These quarries belong to specific clans and they must be compensated either in cash or beasts, buffaloes and pigs, to obtain the rights to dig out the stones. In present days, people often save on costs by just using concrete slabs. Specialist stone-cutters have to be hired and compensated duly in kind, which again means pigs or buffaloes, or cash. Once the stones have been cut, they may be left at the quarry for many years for want of resources to move them to the village.

One of the highlights of tomb building is the process of carrying the stones back to the village and this part involves the most resources. Many cheapskates just rent a truck to bring over the heavy slabs of stones but the traditionalists would have none of these. The rich and powerful would also never consider trucks, for who can miss, if they can afford to, to create a spectacle of over a thousand men using vines to pull giant slabs over wooden rollers for a week, accompanied by men singing and motivating the pullers along the way, and feasts for the hired hands each day. Villagers along the way watch such manoeuvres in awe and they ask, "Whose family is building this?" That's the stardust moment of life in Sumba.

Once the stones have been assembled at the final destination, they are washed with coconut water and a specialist stonecutter is hired to carve in the buffalo or mamuli on the capstone. Rituals, feasts and animal slaughters continue during this and finally one has a tomb worth dying for. If a tomb is already available with enough space, then it's just a question of moving a small door by the side of the tomb and putting in the new dead body.

Daniel said that we were really fortunate to have come when someone had died. He warned us, "It will be very bloody. But you will be okay. You are Asians. Many Westerners turn away when the animal is slaughtered; some even puke or leave the place in anger. But you will be okay. You are Asians."

The patriarch of the household where we were attending the funeral, was a man who had come to Sumba from Flores as a government official and had later married a woman from Sumba. His mother had died from natural causes two days ago. She was argueably a hundred and five years old. Since the family was rich, they had already planned for her eventual death many years ago and had built a tomb beside the house. This was common in Sumba to build a tomb for oneself or someone else in the family who was still alive, again for the reason of sending a social signal.

We arrived early in the morning and there was already a crowd. It was a modern house with brick walls painted in grassy green and with a tin roof, surrounded by a garden compound. Tarpaulin canopies had been set up in the compound as well as the small grass field in front of the house, across the street. Rows of plastic chairs were getting filled up. An area for cooking and serving food had been set up behind the house. We were soon ushered inside and a phalanx of women dressed in traditional ikat sarung and green silk shirts came to greet us one by one. Their way of greeting on such an occasion was to touch their nose with our nose while musicians outside the house played gongs. We saw the dead body, small, covered in plastic wreaths. Some of the older females embraced us lightly and gave us *sirih pinang*. It should have been a sad occasion, but our lack of emotion and fleet footedness didn't seem to cause any raised brows for the hosts. The family was Catholic and she would also have a Catholic funeral before the traditional rites. The head of the house came up to us, shook our hands and asked us to sit at the grand wooden sofa placed in front of the house, along with the *Kepala Desa*, and the *Rato*, the *Marapu* priest. It was the place to seat the most important visitors and there was definitely some social messaging in the display of foreign visitors in that place.

On Daniel's advice, we made a small donation as a gift accompanying our visit. More guests began to come in and they would all shake our hands before going in to see the body. Since the *Rato* and the *Kepala Desa* were constantly smoking, it was becoming difficult for us to play the role of the Guests of Honour and we walked away on the pretext of having a look.

Many children had turned up for the event and were busy with the games. Big jars of cookies had been placed at several points. Sweet tea and coffee without milk was being served frequently. The gong ensemble, half of them women, played whenever they felt like. Many men came over to greet us and ask about us. We realized soon that there were smiles all around. This was not such a sad occasion after all!

After a few words of introductions, the men began posing for photographs. There was a *Kepala Kampung* from a nearby village, another *Rato* and a Mr Busybody. They all sat elegantly with their turbans, known as *kapote*, sarongs and *parangs* or machetes hanging by their waist. I was dressed like them as well while Lobo was dressed in the traditional ikat sarung. Daniel had charged us a good few dollars for this. My *parang* had been coated in oil as was its elaborately carved case. I was wondering how convenient it would be to grip an oily *parang* while fighting. Perhaps to take revenge on me, he had tied my turban tight enough to shrink my skull like Andean people used to do with their victims. The whole day I kept tugging the turban here and there to give comfort in turns to spots in my head.

The funeral events in Sumba are as much about the rituals as they are about waiting in slumber or gossiping. Nothing much would happen for hours and then suddenly we would hear an approaching van or lorry. Then the ensemble came back to life. The gong players began moving their hands again. Our heart beated a trifle faster in anticipation. The lorry was fully loaded with people hanging from its sides. As it approached nearer, young men from the house of the deceased came out in formation. One of the families related to them had arrived. As soon as they got down from the lorry, the men from their group rushed to the front to confront the other group of men from the host's side. Both groups began jumping on one leg as they took out their *parangs*, brandished them horizontally towards the other group and started squealing Arab women cries, "ka ka ka ka." This was a brief interaction after which the women from both groups, the visitors and the hosts, came out to face each other. They were all dressed in the best ikat and began dancing in gentle moves in front of each other. Then the nose touching happened and the visitors gave ikat as gifts to the hosts. The men from both groups climbed up the back of the lorry. They were trying to get down a fattened pig that had been brought in by the visitors. These visitors were not the closest relations and that's why they had brought a pig instead of buffaloes. The pig seemed to be fully aware of Sumbanese customs and tried its best to protest from coming down. The whole group of people who had come for the funeral got up and surrounded the pig. The pig's short legs gathered all the force stored in its fat to resist and it turned round and round; but in the end, there were too many men around it. It fell with a damp thud on the street and was then dragged to the grounds across the street. It squealed, one of those asthmatic heart-wrenching squeals that only pigs are capable of unleashing, as if they knew what awaits them. Once it was tied to a tree, we all returned to our initial positions and the wait began again.

After thirty minutes, another lorry approached. This time, it was a bigger group of visitors led by the host's brother-in-law, one of the most important relationships in Sumba culture. The gongs began, followed by men from both sides brandishing swords and squealing followed by the women's graceful dancing and gift exchanges. But this time there was a buffalo involved, its horns and forehead decorated with shiny red cloth with a golden border. The buffalo must have never looked so good in its life. Unlike the pig, the buffalo didn't resist and followed whichever direction it was pulled at. What gave it such equanimity? Everyone calmed down again.

The next van to come really raised some commotion; it was the water van with an anaconda hosepipe. Rows of seats had to be removed as it sought a nice parking place. A van full of people in khakis appeared soon after. For once, I wondered if they were the police seeking to stop this ceremony which was expected to turn gruesome. But they were only colleagues of the host who were wearing khaki because that was the day for wearing khaki according to Indonesia's government employee charter where each day of the week is associated with a particular colour of uniform, a very useful way to remind the general population what day of the week it was in case they didn't have a reference.

Visitors kept pouring in, finding a place to commence their waiting. By two past noon, four pigs and seven buffaloes had been assembled, each tied to a tree. All the buffaloes had those magnificent red turbans with overflowing sideburns. The largest of them stood out from the rest; it was of a pinkish hue compared to the grey of the rest.

We became the centre of attraction and people came in batches to talk to us. Everyone was looking at us hoping to catch a blink, rewarding us with a humble smile in return. Those who had already introduced themselves dragged in people they considered important, ones we should get introduced to as well, teachers, government officials, and village elders. Women, as everywhere during our trip, gave us their babies to hold. A baby cried immediately upon contact with me, later finding solace in Lobo's lap.

A dozen kids surrounded us, between the ages of two to ten. They also began asking us the usual questions, "Are you married? Do you have children?" We asked them if any of them wanted to come with us to Singapore. This question started a riot. Taking turns, they would gang up on someone and throw him or her in front of us, "Take this one to Singapore." They ran all around playing catcher and victim. One of the older girls was carrying a two year old baby and this baby became a particularly popular choice for sending over to Singapore. But whenever the gang would pull her leg or hand, her sister protector would raise her hand to slap.. She never got too angry; perhaps enjoying all the attention this was drawing to her.

The gang of children was becoming rather noisy. We were getting concerned whether we were violating the seriousness of the occasion. But when we looked around, we could clearly sense that all the patient waiting for action was fast leading to irreverence. Men had formed small groups to play cards. Women had taken to loud chattering. Barrels of tea and coffee were making rounds. One of the pigs had already dug for itself a comfortable pit and lay in it, dreaming of grub. Another was getting excited seeing a female tied next to it. The buffaloes had taken to ruminating.

Daniel had left us on our own and we were happy. We were walking around from one spot to another. Seeing an opening, the men of our age surrounded us. Till now, they had been just looking at us from a distance. They were handsome with their *parangs* and turbans. Many had shoulder length hair, giving them a warrior feel. They tried to discuss Bollywood but their knowledge was far superior to mine, "You know that actress, Aishwarya Rai? She has become three times her size after marriage. How could she do that?" they asked us all a few times. They took us to the front of the house and told us that the action would begin soon. And so it did. Before they left, they asked us to take good pictures of them.

They brought out the pigs first, in a line, like a funeral march. The pigs began squealing again. Some men and women got up from their seats and lined up along the road. The buffaloes looked up calmly to see what was happening, their tails chasing the flies. The pigs were killed even before we realised what had happened. A quick low shove from the parang, pushed through each pig's heart. Even the pigs seemed unaware that they were dying. They looked around but couldn't find any blood. Were they wondering if they had been bitten by mosquitoes? One by one, they fell.

The elders rushed in, grabbing bunches of dry grass. These were spread over the dead pigs and lit, a cremation of sorts. The young men now turned to us and asked us to take their pictures, posing against the burning pigs, the tips of their machetes against the smoking pigs. One of the elders took charge and hacked the pigs to pieces. Others helped him by carrying the chunks, some to the garbage bin, the puddles of intestines; some to the kitchen behind, the meat and the fats. The younger men came back to us to tell that the real deal was yet to come.

Things calmed down again and nothing seemed to happen. We began chatting with the elderly women. Two of them, Ibu Theresa and Marie, were married to the same man and still seemed to be best of friends. They too wanted their pictures and gave us their address. They would share the pictures with the whole village. They said that food would be served soon and we should eat together with them.

Announcements were made over a microphone and a quick queue formed. Ibu Theresa and Ibu Marie dragged us along with them. Daniel suddenly sprang up from somewhere, broke the queue and went in to the front. He asked us to join him but we stuck to our friends. The serving place was rather small for the assembled crowd. It was dark inside. Two rows of high benches had been set up with the food in big aluminium pots. As we got nearer to the food station, the mass took over from Ibu Marie and Ibu Teresa. One hand from somewhere gave me a plastic plate, another shoved a spoon at me. From somewhere, someone dropped a ladle of yellow colored rice on my plate; from the left someone poured a salad like mixture with a tomato overdose. A few servings of pig meat soup were served by different people. "This is the best", said one, "take more, take more", heckled another. We looked around for Ibu Theresa and Ibu Marie but failed to see any faces in the squeezed-in crowd. There were thin potato fries, Chinese style vegetable mix, and diluted sweet syrup for drinks. A man kept talking over the PA system asking people to keep moving. As we emerged from the suffocating enclosure, two young girls led us back to the area where we were sitting before and asked those already seated there to get up. We were informed that there was a separate sitting and serving area for the Muslim guests across the road. They were served goat meat instead of pig meat. Elders kept coming to us asking if we needed anything. The young girls came back with another round of the syrup drinks. When we were done with our food and appeared to be looking for a place to keep the used plates, these girls again sprang up from somewhere. We were feeling almost apologetic for making the villagers attend to us to this extent.

Barely had we finished the food that we noticed that the crowd was getting up on their feet. One of the elder busybodies, Desmond, who had by now become familiar with us came and dragged us to the road. "The sacrifices will begin; make sure you get the best pictures," he said. He addressed Lobo, "Stand behind him. It can be dangerous."

The crowd lined up along the street, shoulder to shoulder, back to front. Fathers held up their boys over their shoulders. The older children climbed up the trees to have a better view. An air of commotion was building up. The pressure of the crowd was building behind me. On the other side, an opening formed in the crowd and about fifteen men assembled around the buffalo tied at the very end. They untied the rope from the tree and began pulling it towards the road. The crowd began yelling. Some broke ranks to give a push to the buffalo to prod it along.

Some took a bamboo to beat it on its back. The hapless animal obliged and ran as directed. It was positioned on the road, right in front of the house. One more rope was put on its neck. A group of people encircled the buffalo. One man held it by the rope on one side; another went to the opposite site holding the other rope. The crowd quickly formed a circle around it. I felt as if the whole world radiated from where the buffalo was standing.

The buffalo swung its head to one side to make sense of things and then the world came to a standstill. Nothing moved and no one said anything. Everyone was watching the buffalo. Reassured, the buffalo calmed down, lowered its head to search for grass on the road; its tail began to wave again. Then a man with an uncovered *parang* slowly walked up to its side. But the buffalo had taken to trusting humans who had been taking care of it well this far. Desmond began giving me live commentary, "Only the very best and most experienced are allowed to strike the buffalo with the parang. It is very risky. What if the blow cut the rope instead? The released buffalo could then maul many to the ground even killing the young ones. What if he hit the horns instead? So humiliating. There has to be a nice clean strike, straight at the jugular." Such a powerful animal with such a vulnerable throat!

And so the man charged in, a quick blow, right on the jugular and he withdrew back into the crowd. People began shouting, "Watch out!" A misty fountain of blood was oozing out. And then there was a drain of blood, a small waterfall. The buffalo took two seconds to realize what had happened. It pulled in one direction and many people joined in to pull the rope against it. It tried to surge ahead and again people pulled the rope from both sides to keep it still. Four men moved forward and began jumping in front of it in one leg, brandishing their swords and making that squealing noise, "ka, ka, ka, ka, ka". The crowd around the buffalo had become fluid by now; moving left, forward, backward, right, following the movements of the wounded beast. It gasped for breath and its blood gushed out in a mist. Desmond was following me, "Take a picture now, did you get it, now, now, get a shot of its eyes!" A young girl squeezed her way to the front and stood beside me, holding her mobile phone to get a picture. I realized that everyone was taking pictures. I looked back and saw Lobo, a little shocked, but hanging on to her position in the crowd to get a decent enough view of what was happening. Another man approached the buffalo to make a gash. The jumping and squealing men doubled their intensity, "ka ka ka ka ka". The mother of the young girl competing with me for pictures came out from somewhere and gave her a tight slap, "Why are you getting so close?" People kept screaming and spitting the red *sirih pinang* mix. The coconut trees by the road, on top of which some children had positioned themselves for the view, were swaying from the movements of the crowd, dangling the children with them. The buffalo fell on its front knees. The road in front had turned red and wet. The buffalo slumbered on one side and was quickly dragged away from the road on the grounds facing the house. The flies that had been circling it all its life finally got the chance to dig in to its blood.

Almost instantly, people rushed in to get the second buffalo. It was caught by surprise. Trying to look into the eyes of the people in front, its eyes looking innocent and tender with its big eyelashes, it rushed in to the arena of death. It occupied its place in the centre, seemingly unaware of the blood of the stranger on the road. The crowd surrounded it and then became still again. A new person took up his pose, ready to strike. But there was a distraction, a motorcycle was approaching. The crowd had to disperse and the buffalo had to be moved back from the road. As the two men on the motorbikes slowly passed through the blood, they exchanged giggles with everyone. The buffalo was moved back to its rightful position and a different man sneaked in slowly to give it the strike. The chain of events was repeated and again the young girl came in from somewhere to take the pictures. What would she grow up to be? The male warriors jumping and squealing in front of the dying buffalo seemed to be trying to communicate with it. But the buffalo wanted to get over with the action; cameras were clicking all around it; we were trying to capture every moment. Desmond kept encouraging me, "Nice one, get one more, now, now once more, come come, come closer." I realized my heart was beating fast. If I got a *parang* to my neck, there would be fountains and mist too. My heart was ready to put on a show. My conscientious vegetarian ideal was protesting but was being shut up by the enormous weight of tradition around me. Some babies had begun wailing; they were quickly dispatched to the back with their mothers. One old man in the front was still finishing his food. The Muslims didn't join the action and were sitting quietly in their halal area. After a series of blows, the buffalo's neck was almost falling off. The buffalo managed to retain it as it fell sideways. Fine red spray came out of its neck whenever it tried to breathe. It was almost beautiful. I was gasping for breath. Lobo was right behind me; speechless. She would hang on and watch it all. As a final gesture, the buffalo tried to move around its neck. Rather loose, it rotated on its broken axis, the buffalo had one last look at the world; it could only have seen the people around it, perhaps me, and collapsed.

The third into the gallows was the special buffalo, the pink beast. It was also the largest. Once it took its place at the centre, its eyes seemed to throw out suspicion from under the thick eyelashes. It didn't put its head down unlike the other buffaloes before it. "This one is strong, this one will be good," said Desmond. I looked over the crowd and saw the other buffaloes nonchalantly going about their business of ruminating. A lean middle-aged man with a moustache positioned himself beside the buffalo in a sideways manner. "It's not looking down, it will be risky, that guy is the best to do it," said Desmond. The man turned his head slowly to look at the buffalo, and then in a quick moment of life, turned and struck. A river opened out and it began flowing buckets. The buffalo didn't move for a while. Everyone remained silent in anticipation. Even the *parang*-brandishing dancers restrained their urge to dance. Then suddenly the buffalo pulled. It dragged the half a dozen men tugging one of its ropes to the other side of the road. The dancers came out and screamed "ka ka ka ka ka". The crowd almost broke up with the women and children rushing out. "This one has so much life!" screamed Desmond in excitement. He was laughing. If it escaped, could the buffalo manage to live like this? It began pulling on the other side now. A brave man jumped in and gave another blow; another river joined in. The buffalo tried to jump. The ropes pulled it down again. "Ka ka ka ka ka," the wailing was deafening now. Another blow from somewhere. But the buffalo kept pulling in all directions. The crowd closed in, their hands raised taking pictures with their phones. "Get its expressions!" cried Desmond. The buffalo calmed down again and stood still. It began to shit, its last shit. Then it pulled, blood was flowing out of its giant nostrils. Its eyes were becoming softer, helpless. It fell on one side, on the road. It was dragged away from the road immediately, over its shit that got levelled into a fine long strip of paste. People left it to get the next one. But it was still alive. Its eyes started to move upwards, it was struggling to keep the eyeballs focused. Two white dogs stepped in to the road to lick the blood. The buffalo's tail flicked once to chase the flies. Its legs trembled suddenly as if it was peddling a bike. Then its head fell, its eyes looking at the sky, lifeless.

Desmond went through my pictures and was delighted. He brought in a few of his friends to see them as well. The crowd began to go back to their seats. We were losing interest in death. The remaining four buffalos seemed to realize this. Without offering much resistance, they came on the road, took the blow, and fell quickly. One even walked itself, after taking the blow, to the place where the others were resting, to fall dead, neatly next to the other dead.

It was over, my heart was calming down. My ears were opening up again. Lobo was back at my side. Daniel joined in, "Wait for a while. The meat will now be distributed among all of us. This is the most important part of the ritual." We didn't go to see how the buffaloes were being dismembered into supermarket meat. We saw people walking around with big chunks in their hands. Some hung this meat on tree branches and walked back to the chopping centre. Our names were called over the microphone and Daniel sprang to get two packets of meat on our behalf.

Desmond came in to explain, "We believe that the blood spilled in front of the house of the deceased makes smooth her passage to heaven. The slaughtered animals will actually join the dead in heaven. Why else would we sacrifice these animals on which we have spent our lives rearing them? We barely eat meat. It's too precious and expensive to eat every day. So we wait for the days of the feasts and the meat is shared with the whole community." That surely put into context the violence we saw with respect to the productivity driven, optimised, and target monitored violence of meat processors in the land of supermarkets. But did the Sumbanese take revenge on nature for death by unleashing more death on nature?

Suddenly there was wailing. Grief had come at its appointed time. The body was being brought out. Around the crying women, there was a stagnant pool of silence. Young girls came out of the house holding huge wreaths of paper flowers. Desmond informed us that there were actually two bodies. The other belonged to the son of the host, who had died three years back at the age of one. A catholic priest was finally given his moment but the rites were quick and simple, a few utterings.

The tomb had been waiting with an open mouth, wooden poles balancing its capstone. It was a simple concrete tomb and the capstone was thin but Desmond confirmed that the family had put on quite a show and we must excuse the fast food nature of this tomb. The bodies were interred for their longest sleep and the lid put over them by twenty men. Daniel rushed us to leave; he kept our share of the meat with him. We didn't get a chance to say a proper goodbye to the many new friends we had made; even Desmond was busy with something else. But we had the address of Ibu Theresa and Ibu Marie. Hopefully they would reply to our letters.

As I rode back to the hotel on Daniel's bike, my ears were shutting out his words. I was thinking about the day, the blood, and the people we met. Was there any inner layer to the obvious conclusions one can draw from the Sumbanese rituals and their fights? The Sumbanese, at least the people who had assembled at the funeral, were extremely dignified, polite, gentle and respectful. They wanted to make us comfortable. They were curious to know more about us and the places we had come from. Unlike many conservative societies, they didn't look at us as immoral tourists, but as their guests who need to be respected and never to be exploited. Especially for a female traveller like Lobo, it is not too uncommon to find local men making insinuations. But not so in Sumba, where everyone treated her and us with utmost dignity. There were too many layers to a Sumbanese, a visible layer, shaped from poverty and harsh weather, a penchant for visual displays of violence, a history of bloody communal fights, stiff and rigid norms of society codified for ages, draining lives without pause; and then there were the same faces that put down all their armoury, bravado and rigidity with the humblest of smiles, which they were ever ready to display, even if stained with a murky betel red.

Afterword

Once we were back in Bali, we were brought back to the reality of a giant protected reserve for tourists with infinite stretches of neatly packed boxes of shops with glass facades, mannequins looking out of them with their contemptuous looks. After days with heart shaped toilet buckets and dim hotel lights, I was fumbling with toilet papers and getting blinded with night lights. But adjustments came fast and soon Sumba and Flores were mixing up in my dreams. For nights, I kept dreaming of countless severed buffalo heads floating around in a blue sky, a crazy smile on their faces. I dreamt of Komodos standing up on their tails and turning the earth with their hands like kids playing with globes; I saw ourselves standing on the Pelni deck overlooking the lakes of Kelimutu which were burping out waves of yellow butterflies; and in a fine blue sea, fat pigs were chasing flying fish and swatting them with their skinny tails.

Daniel kept messaging us offering to take us for a new package tour every day; he was yet to realize that we were a few hundred kilometres away from his hungry wallet. Mama Mena of Bajawa kept messaging me asking about our health and telling us that all the ladies in her stretch of Pasar Bajawa were talking about us every day. Chicken Uncle of Waingapu messaged us asking if we had already sent the pictures, getting anxious as the mail failed to show up at his address that just said, "John Kumis at Pasar Ayam, Waikabubak."

Waikabubak, Waingapu, Waikelele, Waitabula, Waitabar; all those names with Wai that meant water; just like in other Polynesian languages like those used by native Hawaiian and Maori people; a remarkable connection from antiquity; so one town meant water that was boiling; another meant water that was blue; I was fast forgetting which was which.

Did the trip matter to us in any deeper way than any other holiday? Of course, there was the pleasure of not being reachable by my superiors in office, what with the erratic mobile connections in the remote places, but a lingering worry was that they were also not bothering to contact me; was I turning irrelevant? And then, Lobo and I figured out that we could tolerate each other just enough to get married. Besides these, it was invigorating to come up close with those traits of human nature that is usually suppressed in more petrified environments; the trust of strangers, the simplicity, and the fear of death. I was still floating on a pool of unfamiliar collection of myths, whether lakes full of dead souls, or komodos that were actually siblings of humans, to create a fascinating world of tender stories standing softly on a cold base of otherwise rational explanations.

Nonetheless, I was struggling to find big metaphors for our trip. There was no event that I could think of as life-changing, the ones much loved by application forms of those elite business colleges. I flipped through the pictures we had taken, hoping for some clue, something to brag about in brief, without earning a confirmed reputation of opprobrium. Out of the thousands we had taken, warm and radiant, occasionally with a dazzle of blue, there was one, not brilliantly framed, where the parang was an inch away from the buffalo, well on its way to tear off its veins in the next millisecond. With its eyes closed, the buffalo seemed to be anticipating the blow. It was alive at the moment, but a blink of an eye away from irreversible death. I knew what happened after that. But it was what it was at that moment. That moment had excited me, just as Daniel had said that Sumbanese funerals were exciting. But that moment had passed, the buffalo had died. The stars that we saw in numbers we had not heard of before, even they would go through their own individual moments from where they will fall into an irreversible decay. The Komodos would give in one day too, slowly wiped out by some predator or ecological change or by a sudden strike by the meteor or crazy weapons. Even the lakes of Kelimutu, full of the spirits, good and bad, would disappear one day, swallowed in by tectonic forces or a sudden outward eruption. All along the roads we had taken, there was smell of death and rot, a flattened frog, long dry; a puppy that had been just run over, its mashed head a gooey red; a dead rat, thrown around by jumpy crows. In between all this transience, I was finding it tempting to be part of a myth, a realm where one can become an ancestor and stay as such for infinity, watching everything, feeling everything, remaining real, in memories and consciousness of everyone yet to be born, even if diluted in identity, but still not extinct till mankind became extinct. But even being a part of this myth was under threat, from secular rationality, from collective wisdom of organized big religions, from the stigma attached by the media, and simple economics which made ancestor veneration seem too expensive for its value. I hoped this world might linger around just a bit longer, only for me, to feel a little more permanent. I was being selfish for I had moved on, and these people of Sumba and Flores would also move on. Who was I to ask them to not put a mall around the Kelimutu lakes or to not abandon their elaborate traditional homes for Bahaus brick blocks with French names? But for now, I just wanted to dream a little bit more, soaked in this wet, wild world, where strangers walked around me in silence, watchful that nothing disturbs me, from this magical peace.

About the author

Shivaji Das was born and brought up in the north-eastern province of Assam in India. He graduated from the Indian Institute of Technology (IIT), Delhi, subsequent to which he completed his post-graduation from the Indian Institute of Management (IIM), Calcutta. He is presently working as a management consultant in Singapore. Besides travelling, Shivaji also takes an active interest in migrant issues and eradication of underage poverty and is associated with Singapore based organization Transient Workers Count Too (TWC2).

http://www.shivajidas.com

Made in the USA
San Bernardino, CA
09 May 2017